*The
English
Aristocracy*

An evening party at Wanstead House, home of Viscount Castlemaine. By Hogarth.

The English Aristocracy

Marion Yass

"English history is aristocracy with the doors open. Who has courage and faculty, let him come in." Ralph Emerson.

WAYLAND PUBLISHERS LONDON

IN THIS SERIES

English Life in the Seventeenth Century
English Life in the Eighteenth Century
English Life in the Nineteenth Century
English Life in Tudor Times
English Life in Chaucer's Day
Roger Hart
The Search for Prosperity
Richard Garrett
The Cost of Living in Britain
Leith McGrandle

FORTHCOMING

Immigration to Britain Colin Nicolson
The Growth of Literacy in England Christine Wiener
The English Servant Roger Hart
The English Soldier Matthew Holden
The English Sailor Richard Garrett
The Edwardians Christopher Martin

Copyright © 1974 by Marion Yass
First published 1974 by
Wayland (Publishers) Ltd
101 Gray's Inn Road London WC1
SBN 85340 336 8

Printed in Great Britain by
Page Bros (Norwich) Ltd, Norwich

Contents

	Introduction	7
1	The Feudal Aristocracy	9
2	Overmighty Subjects	21
3	Under the Tudor Supremacy	35
4	Outliving the Kings	55
5	The Whig Oligarchy	73
6	Survival of the Fittest	91
7	Partial Eclipse	107
	GLOSSARY	117
	TABLE OF DATES	121
	FURTHER READING	125
	INDEX	127
	ACKNOWLEDGEMENTS	128

Introduction

The British are class conscious. They have a great respect for the class system in general and the upper classes in particular. Every year seven million people visit the stately homes to see how the aristocracy used to live. Interest in their current habits is stimulated and satisfied by the gossip columns of newspapers and magazines.

It might seem strange that the upper class or aristocracy of birth should have survived into democratic, twentieth-century Britain. But the idea that all men are equal is quite a recent one. Neither an eighteenth-century magnate nor the head of a middle-class Victorian household would accept that they were equal in the eyes of God. The Levellers, an extreme republican group in seventeenth-century England, provide eccentric exceptions. The social reformers of the nineteenth century were paternalists rather than democrats; and the political reformers of 1832 were more interested in safeguarding their own influence than in any ideals of one man, one vote. A clever child, whatever his background, can now reach the higher echelons of politics or industry via the state education system, university or the trade unions. But in terms of wealth, power and influence all men are now demonstrably not equal. It is only very recently that the aristocracy has ceased to be the ruling class.

Who are the members of the aristocracy? Originally they were the titled peerage, the dukes, marquesses, earls, viscounts and barons and the lower orders of the nobility, the baronets and knights. All five titled ranks of the peerage are entitled to be called "Right Honourable." This is because all peers used to be Privy Councillors. All except the dukes are addressed as "Lord;" but while younger sons and daughters of dukes and marquesses are "lords" and "ladies," the children of earls, viscounts and barons have to be content with "Honourable." Baronets and knights have a mere "Sir" before their name, although a baronet can put "bart." after his. But in spite of these exact hierarchical distinctions the definition of the aristocracy has been blurred by two factors: primogeniture, the practice of inheritance of the title by the eldest son, means that younger sons, while aristocrats, are untitled; and the creation of life peerages has produced titled men who cannot claim to be aristocrats.

The possession of land has always been the real basis of the wealth and influence of the British upper class. Estates and titles were originally granted together in return for support for the crown. The two have remained associated because an entire estate is inherited by the eldest son with the title. Primogeniture not only smudges the boundaries between the titled and untitled, but keeps the large estates of the nobility intact. The emphasis on land as opposed to family has helped the aristocracy. Great estates are easier to come by than noble birth – the only condition required by most continental aristocracies. Whether money was made by legal practices under the Tudors, royal favour under the Stuarts, East Indies trade or corrupt politics in the eighteenth century, or industry in the nineteenth century, it could always be transformed into a stake in the country. After a couple of generations another country gentleman had arrived, ready to receive his honour. If times were hard the fortunes of the aristocracy could always be rescued by a good marriage with a wealthy heiress, whether merchant, Jew or other non-landed family eager to buy acceptance and status.

Since 1066 the aristocracy has been a distinct class. But it has never been a closed society of a few families. The lack of continuity in the British peerage is at first glance surprising. Many eighteenth-century landowners and heads of Victorian families tried to trace Norman ancestors. Without much ingenuity and a little cheating they were bound to be frustrated. In fact only two hundred of today's peerage were created before 1800. By 1802 only seventeen of James I's creations survived in the male line. A third of the medieval peerage had disappeared by the end of the Wars of the Roses. Two or three surviving aristocratic families came over with the Conqueror. The Berkeleys and the Ardens alone can claim pre-conquest ancestors.

But the failure rate of individual families has been overcome by continual infiltration of new blood and new wealth. Long before life peerages came in, the aristocracy had been open to the talents of the entrepreneur, the lawyer and the politician. Emerson wrote that "English history is aristocracy with the doors open. Who has courage and faculty, let him come in." The aristocracy has not only survived but flourished. It has kept in touch with the rest of society. Its younger sons – sent into the world without estate or title – have gone into the church, the army, the professions and the universities. In this way a pervasive old boy network has been built up. Far from withering in isolation, like the French nobility, the British aristocracy until the 1914 war was powerful in many spheres. The technological age, the welfare state and high taxation now make life harder for them. But the contemporary peer – still mixing almost exclusively with his own kind – is not exactly poverty stricken. He often wields much local if not national influence. The British are still well known for both their class distinctions and their aristocracy.

1 The Feudal Aristocracy

The Norman Conquest

TWO THOUSAND chief Englishmen welcomed William, Duke of Normandy, at Berkhampstead in 1066 as their new king. William had fought Harold Godwin as a legitimate rival claimant to the English throne. He did not demand England's crown by right of conquest. He intended to rule his new kingdom as far as possible with the co-operation of the English people, and especially with that of their leaders.

The Anglo-Saxon nobles were a tough breed, concerned solely with preserving and enjoying their own power. William of Malmesbury, the twelfth-century monk historian, described how "The commonalty, left unprotected, became a prey to the most powerful, who amassed fortunes, by either seizing on their property or by selling their persons into foreign countries." The position of the nobles was based on strength, not hereditary right. King Edward the Confessor called them his royal officials; they were in fact independent rivals based on their separate earldoms. The earls, and the other lay lords and great churchmen were called to advise Edward at his Witan. William I likewise called his tenants-in-chief to his *curia regis*, or great council. In it the English earls Edwin of Mercia, Morcar of Northumbria and Waltheof sat with the Conqueror's followers such as William fitz Osbern and Roger of Montgomery. By allowing Waltheof to marry his niece, William tried to unite the English and Norman elements. Nor had he any need to be vindictive towards the English in order to satisfy his Norman and Breton followers: the confiscated lands of Harold's family and the other defeated nobles were enough to meet their demands.

The Battle of Hastings, 1066. After the Norman victory the aristocracy became a distinct class

An early Norman castle

Castles

The first act of the new tenant-in-chief – or baron as he came to be called – was to build a castle. This was his home, but it was designed primarily for protection against the country people who might not welcome their new foreign lords. It also provided a safe central point from which to run the estates. Speed was essential. A large earth mound was dug from a surrounding ditch. It was steep enough to protect the round, timber stockade placed on its summit from fire or battering with boulders and rams. Later, when the baron had had time to allow the

William the Conqueror creates a new earldom

mound to settle, he built a stone keep. The castle consisted of the "motte" – the mound and stockade – and the "bailey" or outer court. The stockade was so uncomfortable with its cramped quarters and the slit windows necessary for defence that in peaceful times the family often lived in the timber outbuildings of the bailey.

The castles did not entirely prevent the rebellions King William feared. He had to put down risings in Exeter, the north and at Ely. The English nobility, decimated by the battles of Hastings, Fulford and Stamfordbridge, now almost vanished. Those who were not executed, like Waltheof, for their part in the rebellions or killed in the uprisings, fled into exile. Some went to Denmark; many more to Scotland. Others went further afield to Byzantium where they entered the service of the Eastern Emperor. By 1086, when we have the record of Domesday Book, only two of the two thousand English nobles who had welcomed William at Berkhampstead still held important tenancies under the king. William's hope of governing through a multi-national nobility had been frustrated. One hundred and seventy Norman tenants-in-chief held the lands of the Anglo-Saxon nobility of 1066. Eleven of them held a quarter of the country – the same area as was held by the church.

The estates of each new tenant did not form one vast tract of land. Robert of Mortain, William's half brother, held nearly all Cornwall but was also one of the three largest landowners in seven other counties. Earl Roger of Montgomery held most of Shropshire, much of Sussex and also had estates in ten other counties. The lord, his wife, family and entire household moved from castle to castle and manor to manor, living off the produce of each in turn. The scattering of estates arose partly because William had to dispose of lands as they fell forfeit to him from rebellious subjects. But it was also a matter of policy: the constant danger of foreign invasion and the problem of poor communications – a messenger could take a week to ride from London to York – demanded that the influence of trusted men should be spread over the country. The new earldoms were set up for the strategic protection of the kingdom. They were not supposed to be the semi-independent princedoms of Anglo-Saxon times.

The Norman Aristocracy

Twenty years after the Conquest a small foreign aristocracy had been imposed upon the English people. The latter were surprisingly unaffected by the invasion. The old estates remained intact; so did the Englishmen's way of life. They cared little who their lords were or whether land passed from one to another, so long as their rights were respected. A peaceful takeover by the Norman magnates was essential to William's success. When he handed out lands to his followers he therefore insisted that existing rights and customs as well as duties should be upheld. The Norman baron lived off his land in the same way as his Anglo-Saxon predecessor had done: the villein still paid for his virgate (about twelve acres) with his labour and produce. In 1272 it was recorded in the manorial rolls at Holkham, Norfolk that: "Hervey de Monte holds 18 acres for 22d [9p] rent at 4 times of payment and 4 hens worth 4d [1½p] and does 3 half days weeding worth 3d [1p] and 3 boonworks [for the baron] in Autumn at the lord's board worth 6d [2½p] and does 1 boon-work with a plough, if he has a horse, ... and carries the lord's corn in Autumn for one day worth 2d [1p] if he has a horse."

Some old English families survived, as well as customs. William encouraged his followers to marry English heiresses. Indeed, as their overlord, he had the right to marry them to whom he pleased. Robert d'Oilli became the husband of the daughter of Wigot of Wallingford. Henry I himself married Edith, the niece of Edgar Atheling. The new aristocracy became to some degree Anglo-Norman.

The new lords treated their tenants neither better nor worse than their predecessors. While giving the Normans credit for the revival of religion in the country, William of Malmesbury describes how they "plunder their subjects, though they defend them from others." Nor were they less violent than men like Sweyn and Tostig, King Harold's sons: "They are a race inured to war and can hardly live without it; fierce in rushing against the enemy; and where strength fails of success, ready to use stratagem, or to corrupt by bribery." The other important contemporary historian, Ordericus Vitalis, shows how the Conquest itself accentuated the greed and factiousness of the Normans.

The Military Duties of the Norman Nobles

The military aspect of his life was by far the most important to the baron. Battles were not usually clashes in open country but sieges of fortified castles. His home, at the centre of his feudal barony, was a fortress and an armoury. He had to be continually ready to ride out to put down a

The lord of the manor, with villeins in background

War was commonplace between feuding lords. Battles were usually sieges, seen here

rebellion or local uprising. The Norman tenant-in-chief held his land from the king for the purpose of keeping the country at peace. Moreover, he held it not as a reward for support but on condition that he provided the king with an army. It was William's great achievement not only to make his Norman and Breton followers the dominant aristocracy in England but to use them to defend his kingdom. With each grant of land the tenant promised to send the king, whenever he should demand them, a certain number of knights. This was called the *servitia debita*. There was no fixed correlation between the amount of land owned and the number of knights to be provided: the baronies of Cainhoe, Odell and Mandeville were valued respectively at £86, £98 and £100; the first sent fifteen, the second thirty and the third sixty knights to the king. Historians have argued for years over the origins of these figures. Some, following J. H. Round, believe they were fixed soon after the Conquest by individual pacts imposed by the king on his lords. Others believe the figures depended much more on old Anglo-Saxon custom. William did not himself introduce the idea that land ownership should involve a military burden. In England there was already an ancient obligation on every five hides of land to provide one soldier (known as a thegn). William's real innovation was to insist that this service should be given through the lord; also that the relationship of thegn or knight to his lord should be permanent. On the other hand, ultimate loyalty was owed not to the lord but to the king. The aristocracy was supposed to be the prop of the crown, not its rival. That is why William ordered 60,000 sub-tenants of his earls to come to Salisbury Plain and swear an oath of loyalty direct to him. It was no part of the knight's duty to fight his lord's battles. Private warfare was punishable by forfeiture of lands and titles.

The *servitia debita* – however it was calculated – gave William an army of over 4,000 men which he had neither to feed nor to arm. It also formed an important new landed class. For the tenant-in-chief could provide his knights in two ways: he could bring men from his estates to live in his castle, arming, training and paying them. Or, more cheaply, he could give them land in return for knight service. He could grant as many of these packages of land – or fiefs – as he owed knights; or he might grant one knight enough land to support five and let him grant sub-fiefs. Several knights were big landowners. As more fiefs were granted they became distinct as a social as well as a military class. Many a late medieval family was proud to trace its ancestry to a Norman knight.

The Norman sheriff, like the knight, was often the founder of an aristocratic family. William I had no wish to disrupt the system of local administration based on shire and hundred. Englishmen witnessed his early charters; his writs were addressed to English sheriffs. But after the rebellions he had to be sure that the sheriff, responsible for local tax collection and justice, was loyal. So men like Robert Malet and Baldwin of Meules who had supported him in Normandy became sheriffs of Suffolk and Devon. The heirs of the sheriff of Middlesex, Geoffrey Mandeville and of Roger Bigot, sheriff of Norfolk, were important

A knight

enough to become earls under King Stephen (1135-54).

The Continuity of the New Aristocracy

So the new aristocracy was formed without undue disturbance to existing ways of life. Its record of continuity is not good. Rebellions led to confiscations. Families like the Mowbrays of Northumberland forfeited their lands to William Rufus and disappear from all records. Estates had to be split up among daughters if there was no son to inherit. The king had the right to take over a barony if a minor inherited; he could compel heiresses to marry. Obstreperous baronies could therefore be subdued by marrying the heiress either to a poor man, or into the royal family. Henry II gave Constance, Countess of Richmond, to Geoffrey, and Isabel, daughter of Earl William of Gloucester, to John as brides.

While individual families succumbed, the aristocracy as a class prospered. The barons created by Henry I (1100-35) were not necessarily the heirs of William's followers. Ordericus Vitalis speaks of the "new men" like Ralf Bassett whom the king "raised, so to speak, from the dust, and exalted above counts and illustrious castellans." The historian Frank Stenton comments: "They were barons because it pleased the king to treat them as such." The term, not yet specific, was applied to the tenants-in-chief, also to the king's household officers. All barons were called to the three full annual meetings of the king's Great Council. It was their job, unlike that of the lesser aristocracy, the knights, to advise

Richard II with the Dukes of York, Gloucester and Ireland

the king. In practice only the few closest to the king attended his more frequent councils where the real decisions were made. The baron was primarily concerned with protecting his own lands and family and increasing his own wealth.

The Power of the Barons

Self protection became even more vital during the struggles between Stephen (1135–54) and the Empress Matilda. Castles sprouted over the countryside. The power of the barons increased because both claimants needed their support. Both in turn bought their loyalty by returning the sheriffdoms and custody of royal castles transferred by Henry to his own ministers. Both created new earldoms. The *Gesta Stephani* describes how Miles, sheriff of Gloucester and newly created Earl of Hereford, together with his neighbouring sheriff "raised their power to such heights that, from the Severn to the sea, all along the border between England and Wales, they involved everyone in pleas and burdened them with forced services." Miles first supported Empress Matilda, then changed sides when King Stephen offered him the earldom. In this he was typical of the twelfth-century lord. It was a case of every baron or earl for himself.

The barons – except for Geoffrey de Mandeville – were more concerned with defending their own estates than conquering those of their neighbours. For this reason the civil war that raged over the respective rights to rule of Stephen and Matilda, though long, did not lay waste great areas of the countryside. Though the king was powerless to enforce peace, men like Ranulf Earl of Chester and Robert Earl of Leicester made treaties between themselves. By the mid-twelfth century the aristocracy was not primarily an aggressive military group. The Conqueror had tried to stop them raising private armies. Henry I had made these even less likely by letting his tenants-in-chief commute the military service they owed him. Instead of sending him knights in wartime they paid him scutage – so much for every shield owed. Henry could do this because the military needs of the monarchy had changed. The dangers of Saxon risings and Viking raids were over; the King of Scotland was a relative and an ally; the Welsh borders were controlled by the Marcher lords. On the other hand, while William of Normandy had had no need for an army on the Continent, the French monarchy under Louis VI was strong and the counts of Flanders and Anjou were Henry's enemies. There was no point in taking expensively trained and armed knights to besiege foreign castles, especially when their term of service might expire before the journey was completed. It was far better for the king to raise money to hire mercenaries, Flemish crossbowmen or Welsh spearmen. Henry II took five scutages in the first eleven years of his reign.

But it was not only the king who felt a pressing need for money. Earls and barons were no longer content to live off their own estates. They wanted to buy the luxuries of sugar, lemons, cotton, damask and

King John grants Magna Carta at Runnymead, 1215

muslin coming into Europe via the trade routes opened up by the Crusades. They wanted money to fit themselves out for these crusades. They did not like it at all when, in 1166, Henry II held an enquiry into the number of enfeoffments made by each tenant-in-chief, to make sure that he was receiving enough scutage money. The revenue and prestige of the nobility had already suffered from Henry's tendency to seize lands in wardship and from the itinerant justices who now took over the shire courts. The sub-tenants could now take their cases to the royal instead of the baronial courts. The barons missed both the easy manipulation of justice and the revenue from fines imposed in their courts. Resentment grew under Henry's sons: Richard and John raised the rate of scutage, aids and fines. The revenue from baronial demesnes – the manors farmed by the lords themselves – was increasing: the demand from the growing towns for agricultural produce and from the Flemish cloth makers for English wool caused a rise in prices. But the barons did not see why they should pass on their profits to the king. Resistance to the crown's financial exactions was one of the main pressures which forced John to grant Magna Carta in 1215. Through the provisions of Magna Carta the nobles were demanding their old feudal rights, not an abstract concept of freedom for all men.

Barons had fought each other under King Stephen, changing sides for personal advantage. When the threat to their rights came from the crown they struggled together against the Angevins. There was as yet no national sentiment or loyalty. But the barons were beginning to feel a sense of class solidarity. By the late twelfth century the great magnates, living on their vast estates and summoned by writ with the bishops to the *curia regis*, felt themselves to be a distinct class, superior to the middle and lesser landlords. There were perhaps a hundred families in this category.

A tournament. The knights fight in honour of the lady

Hunting with a falcon

Henry III (1216–1272) faced a revolt of the barons in 1258

The horses' trappings and knights' armour show which lord the knights served

The new bourgeois in the towns might be wealthy; the king's household administrators might be powerful. But as well as wealth and power the great lords now had a sense of their own nobility. They gradually evolved their own class outlook and – theoretically at any rate – a strict code of conduct. Women were idealized, knights were always courteous and honour was always kept. These chivalric ideas were first described in Chretien de Troyes' tales of the Knights of the Round Table, sung by minstrels all over Europe. They spread swiftly to England and were encouraged by Henry II's Queen, Eleanor of Aquitaine.

A self-conscious elite, the nobility for the first time became a tightly knit aristocratic class. Their growing pride in their ancestry encouraged them to extend the influence of their families beyond their castles and estates: Hugh of Chester and Roger of Shrewsbury founded religious houses; Robert of Gloucester patronized the historian William of Malmesbury. Heraldry gained new significance. The devices or emblems on the armour, horses' trappings and flags of the knights had had the practical purpose of differentiating one lord's men from another's; they now became in themselves a source of family pride.

The Tournament

Heraldry developed with the tournament. These mock battles gave the lords and their knights a chance to practise their skills in the lulls between wars. By the end of the thirteenth century the tournament was becoming more stylized with the introduction of blunted weapons and elaborate rules; but earlier it had been a serious battle with knights charging at each other dangerously on the open plain. The historian

Simon de Montfort

Matthew Paris described a tournament in 1257 in which many knights received fatal injuries. Nevertheless, earls, barons, their sons and their knights enjoyed travelling not only round England but overseas to tourney with each other. The tournaments became important meeting places for the great magnates. For this reason they were unpopular with the Angevin kings, who were always suspicious of baronial conspiracy. Richard I made them legal in 1194 on condition that they took place on five specified tilting grounds. The combatants had to pay an entrance fee ranging from twenty marks for an earl to two marks for a landless knight. A mark was the equivalent of a third of a pound. Considering a skilled labourer earned $1\frac{1}{2}$p a day this fee, combined with the cost of armour and horses, ensured that the tournament would remain an aristocratic pastime.

Henry III (1216–72) had good reason to fear the tournaments as hotbeds of baronial conspiracy. With their growing self-awareness as a class, the magnates believed themselves to be the natural rulers of the country. In 1258, in the Provisions of Oxford, a group of the most powerful barons tried to make the king govern through a permanent baronial council. But the baron's revolt was short lived. After their victory at Lewes in 1264 and the setting up of Simon de Montfort's parliament, they quarrelled among themselves. Moreover, they wanted to get back to their castles and their estates: the hunting season had begun.

Vert and Venison

Deer-hunting was a passion with the upper classes. The forest law preserved the deer and the boar of the royal forests for the king himself. The legal records tell us that Richard Earl of Gloucester was in trouble in 1251 when he pursued a deer over his own boundary into the king's forest. Before he could hunt the animals – or cut the timber – on his own land the earl or baron had to obtain the grant of "vert and venison." And he was jealous of these rights. His own sub-tenants and villeins (labourers) could hunt the hare or the coney (rabbit) but not the deer on their lord's estates. Hawking was almost as popular as hunting. The thirteenth-century baron could often be seen with a falcon perched on his wrist and spent much time, trouble and money on its training.

The Baronial Household

The huntsman and the falconer lived in their lord's castle with all the other domestic and administrative officials, the knights – including the sons of other magnates learning military and social accomplishments – and the baron's family. By this time the important baronial household was a smaller replica of the royal household.

Knights and officials attended the seigneurial council just as their lords attended the *curia regis*. At the head of the lord's council, and his deputy during his absence, was the steward. He was usually an enfeoffed knight, like Richard of Havering who served Simon de Montfort,

The Percy family—earls and dukes of Northumberland
A very old lapsed earldom granted to Henry Percy, marshal of England (above), by Richard II in 1341. During the Wars of the Roses the Percys were Lancastrians. Deprived of their title from 1461–70. It lapsed in 1537, but restored to them by Elizabeth in 1557. Thomas, the seventh earl, supported Mary Stuart and Roman Catholic toleration. Henry, the ninth earl, was imprisoned in the Tower 1605–21, accused of involvement in the Gunpowder Plot. Tenth earl supported Cromwell. Thirteenth earl created duke in 1766. Commissioned architect Robert Adam to re-model Syon House, his seat near London. The seat of the present duke is Alnwick, Northumberland.

Earl of Leicester. He supervized the wardrober – responsible for the great store or wardrobe where all the provisions of the castle were kept and which had once been a cupboard for the barons' robes and a few luxuries. For example, in January, 1265, for a banquet in the King's honour, the steward bought oxen at 45p each, fresh pigs (as against salted or smoked) at $17\frac{1}{2}$p, hams at 7p and sheep at 5p. As it was a special occasion he also bought ten boars, which each cost 48p.

The auditor was another important member of the household. He travelled round the estates of his lord checking the accounts of the various manors and castles in the demesne. The Earl of Leicester's auditor even noted that at Wallingford Castle there was no increase in swans from one of the three nests because the eggs were carried away in the floods. Several clerks helped these officials to keep their accounts.

There were also the almoner who handed out alms and left-over food from the baronial table to any needy cottars; the chaplain, butler, baker, the cook and the laundress, the tailor, nurses and gentlewomen. The outside servants included the marshal, who had the important task of looking after the horses and stables; the carters responsible for transporting the entire household from one castle to another; and the messengers. These were always on the move, keeping the baron in touch with his various castles, especially in times of baronial revolt.

We know a great deal about Simon de Montfort's estates because the household accounts – the expenditure side of the wardrobe accounts – of his wife have been preserved. Although Simon was the leader of the baronial revolt and Eleanor his wife was the king's sister, the Earldom

Dover Castle

of Leicester was not one of the richest of the dozen earldoms of the thirteenth century. His household was typical of the average wealthy baron, abbot or bishop of the time. His whitewashed castles included Leicester, Wallingford, Dover, Odiham and Kenilworth. Like those to which the other barons returned after Lewes, they were strong fortresses, impressive symbols of their power.

Though much improved since Norman times, they were still not comfortable homes. Glass windows were becoming common only by the end of the century; the new hangings and tapestries did not protect the great halls from damp and draughts on winter nights. During a great feast, expensive tallow candles made from animal fat, would be lit instead of the usual smoky rush lights, and a minstrel would be brought in to entertain them. Otherwise the household retired early. Their indoor entertainment was limited to chess or dice games: few had any books, though Simon himself was exceptional in being able to read Latin and in having his children taught by the scholar Robert Grosseteste. The trestle tables in the great hall were dismantled to make sleeping space on the floor for the lesser members of the household. If quarters were too cramped many slept in the outbuildings of the bailey. Knights, guests, children and nurses were on the second floor of the tower, above the Great Hall. The baron and his wife themselves slept in the solar or chamber off the Hall. Their bed was the most elaborate piece of furniture in the castle: a heavy wooden frame laced with leather thongs to support a feather mattress. The linen hangings suspended from poles gave some privacy from the gentlewomen who also slept in the chamber.

The smooth running of the household was the job of the baron's wife. She made sure that all her family and dependents had sufficient tunics, robes and breeches, made of wool, linen or silk according to rank. She supervised the wardrober in issuing the day's provisions to the cook; these would be enough for an enormous mid-day meal of six or seven meat and fish courses and a lighter supper of eggs and cheese. She made sure that enough ale was brewed from the grain brought in from the demesne: the heavily salted and highly spiced meat kept the household thirsty. If her lord was away at court or fighting she had to be capable of supervizing the steward and the complicated financial business of the estate. She entertained the many guests to the castle, carried on a large correspondence, visited her manors and perhaps a nunnery on her estate. In the chivalric songs of the minstrels she may have been a romantic heroine; in real life she had to be an able manager.

The countess' demanding role was hardly matched by her legal position. As her lord's wife she was secure. But as her father's daughter or her husband's widow she was at the mercy of the feudal law. She could not inherit estates intact; she was entitled only to a third of her husband's wealth if he died; as an heiress she might be forced to marry by the king. The old laws of inheritance were enforced in 1285 by Edward I's statute *De Donis*. While the great magnates were becoming a more powerful and self-conscious aristocracy, feudal law was designed to protect the estate rather than the noble family.

Hunting a deer (note the woman)

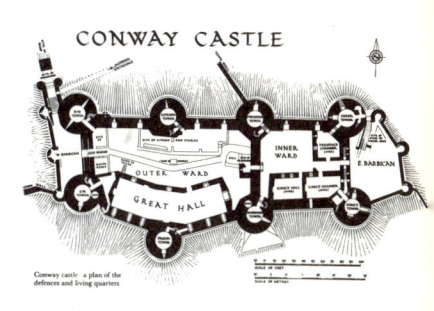

Plan of Conway Castle

Servants preceded by a musician

Noble family at dinner. Only knives are used for eating

John King of France.

The Burgesses of Calais.

Edward III

2 Overmighty Subjects

THE GREAT BARONS of the fourteenth and fifteenth centuries lived in their castles and wore armour just like their predecessors. The likeness was superficial: Simon de Montfort and his followers had gone home to their estates leaving Henry III and Edward I to rule through their councils of royal nominees; the later barons deposed Edward II and Richard II. By the end of the fifteenth century one of them, the Earl of Warwick, was powerful enough to make and unmake kings.

Edward III

The barons resented Edward II's favourites, first Piers Gaveston and then the Despensers. Not only were they foreigners and upstarts but they took up his time when he could have been waging wars. Wars brought valuable booty and ransoms. The nobility also enjoyed fighting for its own sake. It was, after all, what they were trained as youths to do. Like the Black Prince, described by the contemporary chronicler Jean Froissart, they were "never weary nor full satisfied of war ... but ever intended to achieve high deeds of arms." Edward III (1327–77) kept his barons happy, at least temporarily, by going to war with France. They were also delighted with the elaborate tournaments organized by the king at his own expense. Instead of the old, wild mock-battle the tournament was now a series of single combats or jousts fought under elaborate rules. During the next 150 years they became occasions of more and more splendid pageantry. Froissart tells how "King Richard of England and his three uncles ... arranged a great feast to be held at the city of London, where there should be jousts and sixty knights to await all comers ..." The tournament was still the favourite entertainment of the upper class.

Edward III's new Order of the Garter also pleased the barons. Twenty-six Knights of the Round Table – including the king – swore to be "co-partners both in Peace and War, assistant to one another in all serious and dangerous exploits." They wore the blue garter copied from the one dropped by the Countess of Salisbury at a ball, picked up by Edward and fastened round his knee with the words "honi soit qui mal y pense" – "evil be to him who evil thinks." The garter signified "a lasting bond of friendship and honour." The first Knights of the Round Table included the Earls of Derby, Salisbury and Warwick. Edward III won

A joust

Death of Wat Tyler, a leader of the Peasant's Revolt, 1381

A merchant. Under Edwards III and IV many merchants received knighthoods

A squire wearing the livery of his lord

baronial support by linking the popular idea of chivalry with loyalty to the crown.

But King Edward was not to keep baronial support. His long French wars in the end upset the old feudal relationship between crown and nobility. Edward III needed a larger army than Henry II had been able to pay for with his scutages. The old feudal system was obviously inadequate. Other methods had been used in the past. William the Conqueror had paid mercenaries to fight his rebellious barons. In the first year of his reign Edward himself had paid the Counts of Namur and Juliens to raise an army for him in France. He now made individual contracts with his English earls. In return for payment they promised to find, equip and feed specified numbers of fighting men for specified periods. In 1341 several earls provided Edward with an army for Britanny. The aristocracy had become military contractors. They made sub-contracts – or indentures – with lesser men, specifying the strength of the contingent to be provided, the period and place of service, the wages and bonuses, the compensation for lost horses, and the conditions governing the spoils of war such as booty, ransoms and captured castles. In the contracts the magnates left themselves a good margin of profit. They were economical, if not mean, in feeding their troops, often making them live off the land where they fought.

The indenture system with its profits was welcomed by the nobles in a time of agricultural depression. In the 1390s, John of Gaunt asked his council to hold an inquiry into his declining income from land. Conditions varied over the country, but the Percy estates of Cumberland and Northumberland are typical of many: in 1266 the Earl's income was derived entirely from his farm produce and rents in kind. By 1350 it came from money rents. Because their land was not proving profitable many landowners preferred to let it out rather than cultivate it themselves. But the terrible Black Death (bubonic plague) of 1348 and its recurrences brought a dearth of potential leaseholders, and low rents. It also held up commutation in some areas where the lord was loath to lose the few remaining villeins on his demesne. The Peasants' Revolt of 1381 showed how many nobles still treated these men as feudal property.

The French wars helped the magnates to survive the depression. Indirectly, too, they brought new blood into the aristocracy. Edward III had found a new method of raising his army; he now had to find the money to pay his military contractors. Each expedition to France cost about £50,000. Parliament voted subsidies of £38,000. Where was he to find the balance? The Jews had been expelled by Edward I, so he could not borrow from them. The Florentine bankers, the Bardi and the Peruzzi, made him such enormous loans that they soon went bankrupt. Edward then turned to the English merchants, who were making their fortunes from trade in the growing towns. In return for large loans he made them concessions, the most important being a temporary monopoly of wool exports. Many quickly lost their new riches; others, like Sir William de la Pole of Hull and Sir John Pulteney, a member of the Drapers Company, bought estates in the country. De la Pole's son became the Earl, and his great grandson the Duke of Suffolk; the Pulteneys became Earls of Bath. More London merchants were knighted by Edward IV in return for loans. The Wottons, the Boleyns, the Russells bought land, and turned themselves into country gentry. However rich and powerful they were in the towns they could not become part of the aristocracy until they had their stake in the country. The same was to be true of the Tudor merchants and the nineteenth-century bankers. The link with the towns remained: by the end of the fifteenth century it had become fashionable for the great magnates – including the abbots and bishops who built themselves mansions in the Strand – to have their town houses in or near London. But the country estate was a necessary condition for the establishment of a title, and the aristocracy remained an essentially rural class.

The ranks of the lesser aristocracy were also swollen by the wars. Many indentured men made their fortunes from their share of booty and ransoms and from rewards. Edward III gave Audley £400 a year for his services at the Battle of Poitiers. Sir John Falstaff accumulated enough capital to invest in flocks of sheep. He turned Castle Combe in Wiltshire into an industrial manor where he wove and dyed cloth. "In these days," wrote a contemporary, Nicholas Upton, "we see openly how many poor men through their services in the French wars have become noble, some by their valour and some by other virtues that ennoble men."

The contracts made between magnates and men at arms usually extended beyond the end of the fighting. An indenture drawn up between John of Gaunt and Symkyn Molyneux, Esquire on 15th February, 1374, "witnesses that the said Symkyn... shall be bound to serve our said Lord as well in time of peace as of war in whatsoever parts it shall please our said lord, well and fitly arrayed. And he shall be boarded as well in time of peace as of war." The indentures often specified household and personal duties. Sir Thomas Clinton was bound to ride with his lord, the Duke of Nottingham; Philip Darcy to attend Gaunt at Parliaments and assemblies.

A fighting man returning from France was usually very willing to stay within the orbit of his lord. As the power and influence of the magnates grew – especially under the long minority and then the insanity of Henry VI (1422–61) – their protection became more necessary to smaller men. Life became dangerous for a man in the north if he did not belong to the affinity of the Nevilles or the Percies, or for an East Anglian without the friendship of the Duke of Suffolk.

Livery and Maintenance

Indentured men and retainers surrounded each great noble. Some may have been his tenants, but the basis of the relationship was monetary and personal, not territorial. The duke, earl or baron no longer kept the services of his household and administrative officials by giving them land; sub-infeudation had been legally ended in 1295 by the statute *Quia Emptores*. Instead the lord now gave them board and protection

– or maintenance – and the uniform or "livery" of his household. The retainers were instantly recognizable as their lord's men by the badge on their livery: the rising sun of York, the portcullis of Beaufort, the bear and ragged staff of Neville. In 1343 Elizabeth de Burgh, Lady of Clare, had liveries of cloth and fur made for 93 esquires, 15 knights, 39 clerks, 96 household and outside servants, 12 pages and several farmers and tradesmen. Even Sir John Falstaff, newly recruited to the lesser aristocracy, bought hundreds of yards of red and white cloth for liveries for his retainers.

The system of livery and maintenance – now known as bastard feudalism – depended on the demand for "good lordship" or protection in troubled times. Much land was in dispute because of the disappearance of feudal customs. It took time for property law to develop in its place. In the meantime, claims were decided by force, not law. And the great lords were only too eager to step in to their own advantage. The letters of the Paston family are full of their sufferings at the hands of the nobility: in 1450 Lord Moynes grabbed their manor at Gresham; in 1465 the Duke of Suffolk marched on two more manors with 500 men. The family changed its allegiance from the Duke of Norfolk who had patently failed to give them protection, to Lord Hastings. Their old lord then relieved them of Caister Castle.

Jealous of each other's growing power, the nobles were continually involved in private wars. The odd skirmish with a local magnate had the extra advantage of removing the armed retainers from their lord's castle where they could become unruly and rebellious. When the Earls of Westmoreland and Northumberland fought in 1404, the latter was convicted merely of trespass, not treason: so much had the king's authority degenerated since the time when the death penalty had been the punishment for private warfare. Neville continually fought Percy; Lords Grey and Fanhope fought in Bedfordshire in 1437; the Earl of Devon and Lord Bonneville in Cornwall in 1441. Bonneville's councillor had his manor burned and his throat cut by Devon's men. The landed classes lived in an atmosphere of suspicion, violence, murder and treachery. A petition to the king recorded in the Parliamentary Roll for 1459 complained "of robberies, ravishments, extortions, oppressions, riots, unlawful assemblies, wrongful imprisonments," and that the "misdoers be so favoured and assisted by persons of great might . . . that no execution of your law may be had."

Local administration was virtually in the hands of the great magnate. He would appear at the assizes, or county courts, with such an impressive force of retainers that the decision of the court was unlikely to go against him or his men. The justice of the peace, presiding over the quarter sessions, had been a royal nominee from the landed gentry acting for the king. But he was now closely associated with the local lord, probably one of his retainers and in need of his protection. In Warwickshire in 1421 the justice of the common pleas and the justice of assize were both paid retainers of the Earl of Warwick.

In central government, too, the nobles were all powerful. Where

Fifteenth century court of law. Justice was administered by local lords

Richard Neville, Earl of Warwick

Edward I had chosen the barons he wished to sit in his Council, Edward III had accepted the chief magnates' demand that they had a right to be summoned. They became the king's chief councillors: the royal nominees sank to rubber stamp officials. They dominated the Commons through the knights of the shires – their own retainers. By the time of the Lancastrians (1399–1461), aristocratic factions ruled the country through the Council and Parliament.

The plague claimed many aristocrats

Noble Marriages

The balance of power between aristocracy and crown was shifting. There was also a change in the basic relationship between king and nobles. Instead of the feudal overlord, the king was now just another great magnate. Edward III's policy of marrying his children into the nobility was partly responsible for this state of affairs. When John of Gaunt married the heiress Blanche he became Duke of Lancaster. Lionel, Edward's third son, married Elizabeth de Burgh of Ulster and Clare, becoming Duke of Clarence. Royalty was thus involved in aristocratic rivalries. Private wars for land and local influence escalated into the Wars of the Roses (1455–85) with the throne as prize.

The nobles were as careful as the kings to marry off their children profitably. Alliances among themselves were an important means of increasing their wealth and influence. The Neville family provides a good example. Ralph Neville, created Earl of Westmoreland for his support of Richard II, married a daughter of John of Gaunt and created a powerful dynasty through the marriages of their fourteen children. Two daughters married the Dukes of Norfolk and York; three sons became Lords Fauconberg, Abergavenny and Latimer through the inheritance of their brides. The heir married Alice Montagu who brought him the Earldom of Salisbury. Their son Richard added the Warwick title and estates to his inheritance by marrying the heiress of the Earl of Warwick. His power was so great that he could decide the succession between Henry VI and Edward IV.

The availability of these heiresses was due to the failure of many noble families to produce sons. Even when they did so there was a fair chance that the heir might never inherit the title. The infant mortality rate was high, and even higher for boys than girls. Plague and disease claimed their aristocratic victims: it was Henry of Warwick's sudden death in 1447 which left Neville's wife as the heiress. Many sons of noble families, like the Black Prince himself, died in the French wars. Others, including William Montagu, Earl of Salisbury, were killed unnecessarily in tournaments. A chronicler told how, in 1389, "the Earl of Pembroke, a young man not quite seventeen years old, insisted upon trying out his horse with another knight. The Earl's horse took fright and flung him with great force so that the spear entered his body near the groin and inflicted a mortal wound." Only two great families – the Mortimers and the Beauchamps – could boast an unbroken line of male descent from the beginning of the thirteenth to the end of the fifteenth century.

Many old families disappeared as their estates were split up among daughters, while the Nevilles and others increased their wealth. The new men entering the peerage – financiers like the De la Poles and royal administrators like James Fiennes, the chamberlain of the king's household – were far fewer than the families which died out. The great nobles therefore became fewer and richer. By the mid-fifteenth century a mere ten dukes and a dozen earls owned most of the country's wealth. With thirty other lords and the bishops they comprised the upper aristocracy. Their average income, according to the 1436 taxation returns, was more than £3,000 (about £120,000 today) and several were much wealthier. They formed a social elite quite distinct from the lesser nobility or knights whose incomes varied from between £40 to £200. The distinction was preserved by the revival of primogeniture, by which the entire estate and title was inherited by the eldest son, a practice which had lapsed in the previous century.

Baronial Wealth

The great lords needed vast incomes to meet their vast expenses. They had to provide food, liveries and shelter for their followers. A large retinue proved the magnate's powerful lordship, and drew the local gentry into his circle. The Duke of Clarence supported an establishment of 299, the Earl of Northumberland one of 166. Their prestige depended not only on the size but the splendour of their retinues. Attendances at the king's Council or a tournament were excuses for extravagant displays of pomp to impress the gentry, the king and each other. The spirit of chivalry might have been dying but the outward forms were stronger than ever, demanding elaborate trappings and ceremony.

Aristocratic clothes, made from expensive furs, velvets and silks, mirrored the same love of display. A chronicler disapproved of the extravagance: "Englishmen have gone stark mad over fashions in dress. First came wide surcoats that reached no farther than the hips; then others that came clear down to the heels, spread out at the sides to arm's length. They wear also small hoods fastened right up under the chin in womanish fashion... embroidered all about with gold, silver and precious stones. Their shoes which they call crakows have curved peaks more than a finger in length resembling the claws of demons rather than ornaments fit for human beings."

The new fashions owed much to foreign influence. On their excursions to the wars of Edward III and Henry V (1413–22) the nobles could see how the French aristocracy lived. When they came home they copied their furnishings, plate and jewels. They demanded new comforts and luxuries. Some added new halls, as at Berkeley; others built new castles. These were far more comfortable than the thirteenth-century thick-walled fortresses; but many nobles preferred to live in fortified manors

Bedroom in fifteenth century noble household

Entertainment in a noble household

like the one the Earl of Suffolk built at Wingfield. The painter Thomas Hearne commented: "Upon the whole this fabrick seems to have been formed rather to inspire the idea of dignity than to resist an enemy."

Castle and manor alike were built around the great hall. For the lord's followers had to be able to congregate together. Here, overshadowed by the rich tapestries, the nobles entertained lavishly. Their hospitality was showy, designed like their retinues to impress. Apart from the indentured men and household retainers there were always guests for dinner, at 11 a.m., and supper, at 4 p.m. Lay castles and manor houses were open to travellers for food and shelter, taking over the old role of the monasteries. The household accounts of Elizabeth Berkeley, Countess of Warwick before the title passed to the Nevilles, give a detailed list of her guests in the year 1420. She welcomed unknown travellers and hermits, charcoal burners bringing fuel, fish merchants and goldsmiths; a royal messenger bearing a summons to the Earl for the Winchester Parliament; the officials of the Earl's estates and two of his wards; many women friends with their damsels, esquires and valets; and John, Duke of Bedford, brother of King Henry v. who arrived with chancellor, treasurer, twenty-four esquires and forty-two other retainers.

A typical daily entry in the Countess' account lists 46 to dinner and 38 to supper. Together with the lesser domestic servants who ate separately, they consumed 146 white loaves from the pantry; five and a half gallons of red wine and 68 gallons of ale from the buttery; 100 white and 80 red herrings – it was Lent – from the kitchen stores and two haddocks and 300 oysters purchased from the fish merchant. From the wardrobe they used spices from a range which now included mace, cloves, pepper,

The lavish scale of a medieval banquet

When the lord was away his wife travelled from estate to estate to supervise the running of them

ginger, aniseed, pimento, cinnamon and sandalwood. When the Earl came home in March with his retinue the Countess had to provide for six henchmen and nine grooms as well as sixty retainers.

The lord was so often away at war that his wife ran the estates with her husband's steward. The Countess of Warwick was often on the move with her daughters, six gentlewomen, three women of the chamber, nine gentlemen including her steward, two esquires, her usher, cook, butler, valets, laundrywoman, grooms and menial servants. They travelled from Berkeley Castle to the Essex manor of Walthamstow, to Good Rest Lodge near Warwick, and to her other manors. When in England the Earl stayed mainly at Berkeley. Here he supervised the running of the estates and held his council. The importance of the baronial council grew as the magnates consolidated their estates and extended their influence. The duke or earl handed out justice with the advice of his chief household and estate officers, his lawyers, and a few neighbouring lords and knights. In 1485 Richard III's baronial council was effective enough to become the powerful Council of the North.

Education and Learning

The nobles' administrative and judicial roles, and continual law suits over land titles, imply some degree of literacy. They had a better education and a greater interest in learning than the picture of the marauding baron fighting his private wars usually allows. A typical upper-class boy

Educating young nobles

was taught at home by the women and chaplain of his father's household until he was seven. His sisters remained to learn deportment, sewing, singing and dancing. Occasionally, like Isabel the granddaughter of the dowager Countess of Suffolk, sent to the house of Poor Clares at Bruisyard in 1417, they were boarded out in nunneries. The girls gained some knowledge of legal terms and accounts to prepare them for their part in managing their future husbands' estates. Meanwhile the noble boy was sent to the castle or manor house of a neighbouring lord to learn reading, writing, Latin grammar, religious principles and manners according to the chivalric code. The Duke of Northumberland's household in the 1480s included six chaplains and a master of grammar. When he was fourteen the boy became a knight and learned military skills. Very few joined the scholars at the newly-founded schools of Winchester and Eton, but several went after their military apprenticeship to Oxford or Cambridge, now flourishing intellectual centres. These were mainly younger sons destined for the church, like the Earl of Warwick's brother, George. He became Archbishop of York in 1464, an occasion celebrated by the Earl in his London house with six hundred of his liveried retinue and six thousand guests.

Other younger sons of the nobility entered the Inns of Court. They were forced to find an occupation while their elder brothers inherited estate and title. Only the wealthy could afford the expense of legal training at the Inns. Henry v's Chief Justice, Sir John Fortescue, commented: "Hence it comes about that there is scarcely a man learned in the laws to be found in the realm who is not noble or sprung of noble lineage."

New College, Oxford

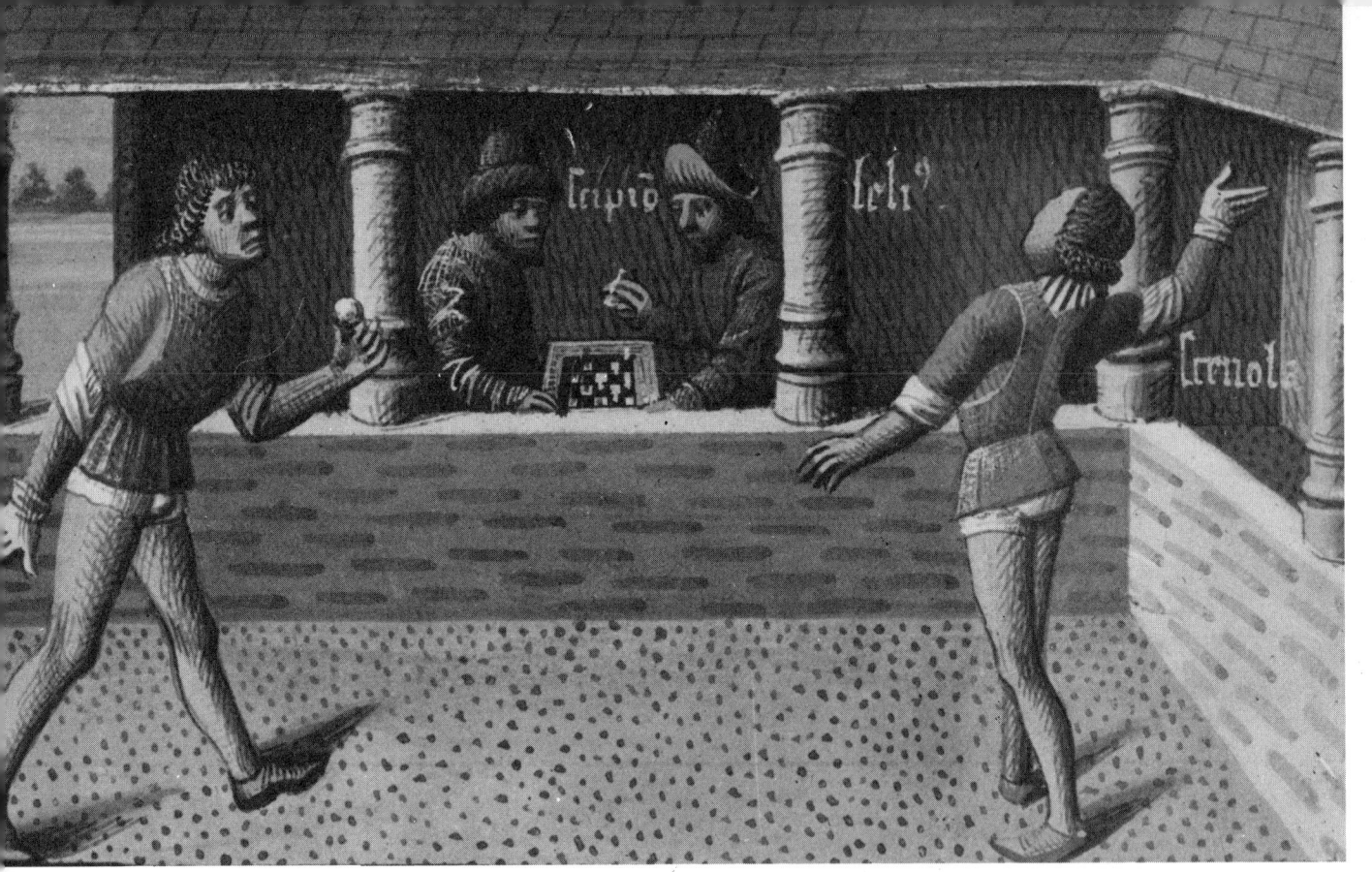

Chess was a favourite game of the aristocracy

Musicians in a noble household

English was replacing Latin as the language of the law courts and parliament. The nobility were now reading and writing English instead of Latin, even speaking English instead of French. Some of them became interested in English writers, using their wealth to give them hospitality and encourage learning. Gaunt of Lancaster supported John Wycliff – though this may have been for his anti-clerical views as much as for a love of letters. The Duke of Norfolk collected books and paid for several

Peasants hunting rabbits. After 1381 hunting was effectively reserved for the aristocracy because to hunt one had to have property worth 40 shillings (£2) or more

of his retainers' sons to study at Cambridge. John of Bedford, Bolingbroke's son, bought more than eight hundred books from the French king's library when he was in Paris; Humphrey, Duke of Gloucester invited Italian scholars to England and bequeathed his valuable library to Balliol College, Oxford.

Literature was a minority taste, but every noble household enjoyed music and acting. The Duke of Norfolk included "Thomas the harper" and several singers among his retainers; the Duke of Gloucester and the Earl of Essex had their own troupes of players. The nobles were happy to let their dependents and tenants share these pleasures and to play them at chess, backgammon – known as "tables" – and cards when they were introduced towards the end of the century. When it came to hunting, however, the aristocracy were less eager to share their enjoyment. One of the demands of the peasants when they rebelled in 1381 was that everyone should have the right to hunt and fish. Parliament – full of small landowners dependent on the protection of great magnates – replied by imposing a penalty of a year's imprisonment on any layman found hunting who did not possess property worth forty shillings (£2). Even in such matters the nobility insisted on its distinctive rights as a landowning class.

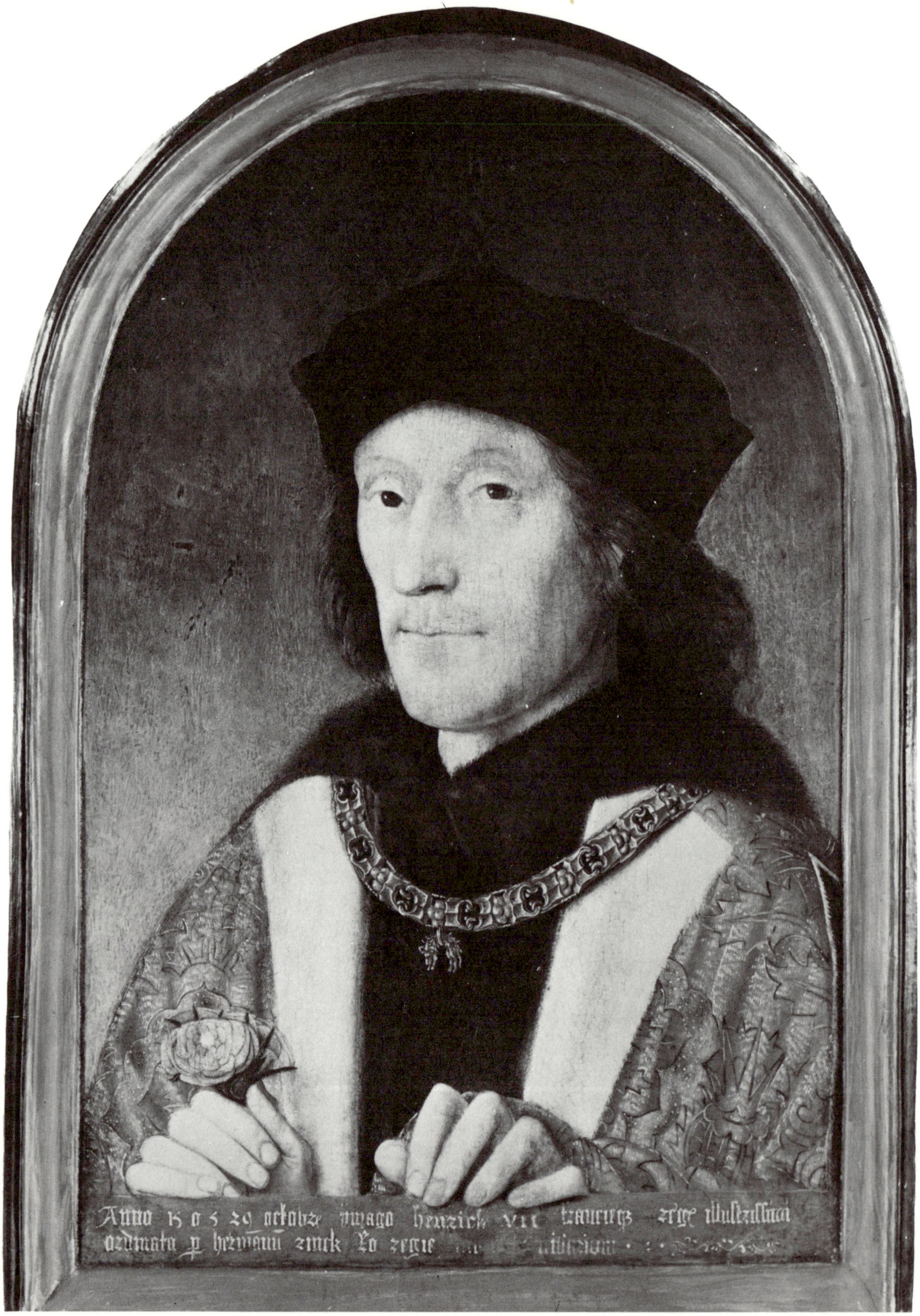

3 Under the Tudor Supremacy

The Contraction of the Peerage

Only eighteen nobles took the oath at Henry VII's first Parliament after he became King in 1485. The depletion of the peerage at the beginning of the sixteenth century has been blamed on the Wars of the Roses. In Sir Thomas More's *History of King Richard III*, Buckingham laments that "in the inward war among ourselves hath been so great effusion of the ancient noble blood of this realm that scarcely half remaineth, to the great enfeebling of this noble land." At the battles of St. Albans, Bosworth and Tewkesbury the Dukes of Norfolk and Somerset, the Earls of Northumberland and Rutland and Lord Clifford all died. Yet the number of lapsed peerages between 1450 and 1500 was no greater than those in any half century since 1300. During these fifty years thirty-eight noble families failed in the male line, but only twelve violently and few of those in the war. The search for sole heiresses seems ironically to have defeated its own end: the weakness of their genes might explain their inability to produce heirs. A few of the nobility who were killed in the fighting in any case had no heirs and no hope of producing any.

Retributions after the war have also been blamed for the extinction of the old nobility. The weapon of revenge was the attainder. This legal action brought not only death to the traitor but the loss of all his goods and estates and the disinheritance of his heirs. Henry VII did not use it indiscriminately. He wanted the loyalty, not the destruction of the Yorkist and Lancastrian nobility. The Yorkist De la Poles only suffered the extreme penalty after intriguing against the new king. Henry VII restored the peerage to 1450 members by the reversal of all but thirteen of his attainders; and only five of these affected the higher nobility. It was the threat of attainder which kept them docile. The Tudors used it for coercion rather than destruction.

Henry VII was not as vindictive as his reputation suggests. On the other hand, he had no desire to redistribute any lapsed titles to new men. During his reign (1485–1509) the peerage shrank from 57 to 44. Nor were those who kept their lives, lands and titles allowed to keep the power of the fifteenth-century magnates. Henry was determined to end the basis of this power: the system of livery and maintenance. The Star Chamber – as his Council was called when it sat in its new judicial capacity – enforced his sumptuary laws against "unlawful maintenance, giving of liveries, signs and tokens and retainers by indenture promises

Opposite Henry VII (1485–1509)

oaths writing and otherwise." A fine of £10,000 was imposed on the Earl of Oxford for exceeding the permitted number of retainers allowed to any lord. In fact the sumptuary laws were gradually forgotten: large retinues reappeared in the 1530s when no lord was seen at a pageant or tournament without his followers; in 1562 the Earl of Oxford was able to drive to his father's funeral with 140 household retainers dressed in special black liveries. But such retinues were now unarmed; they signified social rather than military influence.

Advisers to the King

Political as well as military power was eluding the old nobility. The Councils of the North and the Marches imposed royal authority on the old spheres of influence of the border lords. Even the justices of the peace were brought under the control of the crown. As for Parliament, it was rarely summoned by Edward IV or Henry VII. By the 1530s, when it seemed necessary to have statutory confirmation for Henry VIII's reformation of the Church, members of Parliament no longer depended on the great lords for protection: they did not now constitute a veiled aristocratic threat to the crown. The Great Council of the king's "natural advisers" – the nobility, bishops and higher clergy – was only called four or five times a year for routine business. Real government was carried on through the king's smaller personal council. In 1501 Henry VII's council consisted of nineteen commoners and only thirteen peers.

The monarch's ministers and favourites, advising him in his small council, prospered. Dukes, earls and barons could no longer make fortunes through indentures and foreign wars. The crown had at its disposal not only the lands forfeit by attainted traitors, but also the demesnes of abbeys and monasteries which were confiscated when Henry VIII ordered the dissolution of all the religious orders after his break with the papacy (this followed the Pope's refusal to annul his marriage to Katherine of Aragon). These lands accounted for one-fifth of the whole of the arable land of the country. They were granted to, or bought by, new secular landlords. For service to the crown was rewarded either by great estates or by offices profitable enough to allow the purchase of an estate; and land, as always, was a necessary condition of title. By choosing ministers according to merit rather than birth the Tudors deprived the old nobility of influence and also brought new families into the aristocracy. The Pagets were typical: William Paget's father was a mace bearer in the City of London. After attending St. Paul's School he entered the royal service and rose to become Secretary of State. With his new riches he bought lands which had belonged to the Bishop of Coventry and Lichfield and was given a barony. His descendant became a marquess for his part in the Napoleonic Wars. William Paulet, one of Henry's favourite administrators, became Comptroller of the Royal Household; he was rewarded with Netley Abbey near Southampton and the marquisate of Winchester.

After the Dissolution (1509), many abbeys and their lands were granted to the rising middle class. Malmesbury Abbey, Wiltshire

John Russell succeeded Paulet as Comptroller of the Household in 1537. Russell came from a family of Dorset merchants and squires (see Chapter 2). He began his service to the crown by fighting in the French wars; there he lost an eye and won a knighthood. His insight into financial and administrative affairs won him lucrative export and import licences. As Comptroller he was granted the abbeys of Tavistock and Woburn, a barony and the Earldom of Bedford.

Like the Russells, the Cecils showed how administrative talent and shrewd diplomacy could raise a family from the middle class into the aristocracy. William Cecil's grandfather was a yeoman, his father a page of Henry VIII's wardrobe. He himself became Elizabeth's Lord Treasurer and, in 1571, Lord Burghley. William remained the Queen's chief minister until his death in 1598. Burghley's son, Robert, succeeded him as Elizabeth's chief minister. The manors and lands he acquired in twenty-one years filled six pages of records.

Cecil had to wait for James I to reward him with a viscountcy and then the earldom of Salisbury. Elizabeth I (1558–1603) was not at all generous with titles. Dudley, who became the Earl of Leicester, was one of the very few of her favourites whom she honoured. Others, like Sir Christopher Hatton, Sir Francis Walsingham and Sir Walter Raleigh might have expected peerages. Hatton, the son of a small Cheshire farmer, caught the Queen's eye while dancing in the traditional Inns of Court masque performed at court; he became her trusted Vice Cham-

William Paget, Baron

37

berlain and Chancellor. Walsingham, the son of a common sergeant, and Raleigh, son of a small farmer, also served the Queen well. Although they were given large grants of land they remained mere knights. As a contemporary, Thomas Fuller remarked, the Queen "honoured her honours by bestowing them sparingly."

Nobles and aspiring nobles alike were well aware that their fortunes and even their survival depended on the crown. They looked to the monarch for advancement in the form of profitable offices and estates. Their attitude was very different from that of their predecessors who had seen themselves as rivals to the crown. Their king was not now the most powerful noble but a monarch ruling by divine right. Allegiance was owed not to him personally as a "good lord" but to the crown as

The Cecil family—marquesses of Salisbury and Exeter
David Cecil became a prosperous yeoman and courtier under Henry VIII. William Cecil, created Lord Burghley (above), became Elizabeth I's principal minister and most trusted adviser. His son Robert became Elizabeth's secretary in 1596. In 1605 he was created Earl of Salisbury. His eldest brother Thomas was made Earl of Exeter. Robert built Hatfield House. The family continued to be important politically. The third marquess was Prime Minister in the nineteenth century. The fifth marquess advised Elizabeth II on the choice of Prime Minister after Eden's resignation in 1956.

Robert Dudley, Earl of Leicester

Queen Elizabeth I (1558–1603)

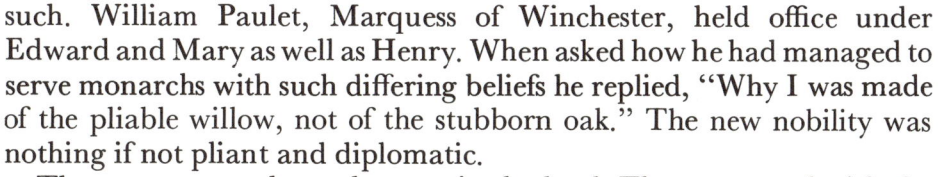

Thomas Howard, 3rd Duke of Norfolk

such. William Paulet, Marquess of Winchester, held office under Edward and Mary as well as Henry. When asked how he had managed to serve monarchs with such differing beliefs he replied, "Why I was made of the pliable willow, not of the stubborn oak." The new nobility was nothing if not pliant and diplomatic.

These men were the real power in the land. They governed with the Queen. Percies, Talbots, Howards and the other heirs of the old aristocratic families were prominent in the social but not the political life of the court. Elizabeth preferred that they should be at St. James's Palace with her, rather than setting up power bases on their country estates. In the north the old economy and the practice of livery and maintenance lasted longest: the Percies, Nevilles and Dacres were not crushed until after the 1570 rebellions. Elsewhere in the counties the duke or earl remained a social focus; but it was the new landowning gentleman who now represented the county at Westminster and acted as the local justice of the peace.

Social Mobility under the Tudors

The country gentry flourished with the wool trade and the rise in prices. They could afford to buy the monastic lands coming onto the market. So could the financiers, merchants and lawyers from the city who now joined them. For they used their riches not to set up commercial urban

Sixteenth century merchants (above) used their riches to buy land. Their children often married into the aristocracy

Queen Elizabeth with members of the aristocracy

dynasties like their German and Italian counterparts but to buy land. The financier, Horatio Palavicino, used the interest on his loans to the monarchy and to courtiers to buy eight thousand Cambridgeshire acres and the position of a country gentleman. The sons and daughters of the new landowners from the towns swiftly acquired "county" status. They married into the existing gentry and sometimes into the peerage. The great granddaughters of William Sturpe, the industrialist who bought Malmesbury Abbey and became a J.P. and a member of Parliament, married the Earls of Rutland, Suffolk and Lincoln.

Movement up and down the social scale and from town to country was easy. But if society was flexible it kept its hierarchical attitudes. Elizabeth snobbishly tried to keep the peerage as a closed caste even though she deprived it of real power. She tried to enforce the sumptuary laws of the early Tudors which regulated the type of clothes worn and food to be eaten by men of different classes. The gentry, once secure, were just as keen to preserve the established order. In Norfolk they were quick to put down the rebellion of 1549, horrified at the suggestion of Robert Kett leader of the revolt, that the peasants should share their prosperity.

Contemporary preoccupation with class and "gentility" showed the insecurity of men unused to the new social mobility. Ben Jonson's character in *Every Man out of his Humour* tells his friend: "I have land and money... and I will be a gentleman whatever it costs me." The new men were eager to prove they were as noble and gentle as the old aristocracy. Lord Burghley told his son: "Gentility is nothing else but ancient riches." To prove their riches ancient the new families needed pedigrees, illustrated in coats of arms, hence the many applications to the herald's office. Shropshire was typical of the whole country: in 1433 it could boast 48 families with arms; in 1623 there were 470. The proliferation was due not so much to the success of the herald in tracing families back to medieval or Norman times, as to his willingness to co-operate. "For money," said a Secretary of State, a herald would give a man "arms newly made and invented, the title whereof shall pretend to have been found by the said herald in perusing and viewing of old registers." Even the most successful newly ennobled families felt the need to bolster their titles in this way: Lord Burghley tried to trace the Cecils back to one of King Harold's followers. In the hall of his new home, Theobalds, he hung a huge map showing the estates and coats of arms of every great landowner in the country.

"Prodigy" Houses

Theobalds, Sir Christopher Hatton's Holdenby, Sir Francis Walsingham's Wollaton and Hardwicke Hall, built by Bess of Hardwicke, the Countess of Shrewsbury, were typical of the "prodigy houses" built by the new nobility. The aristocrat no longer needed a fortress for pro-

Hardwicke Hall, typical of the houses built by the new nobility

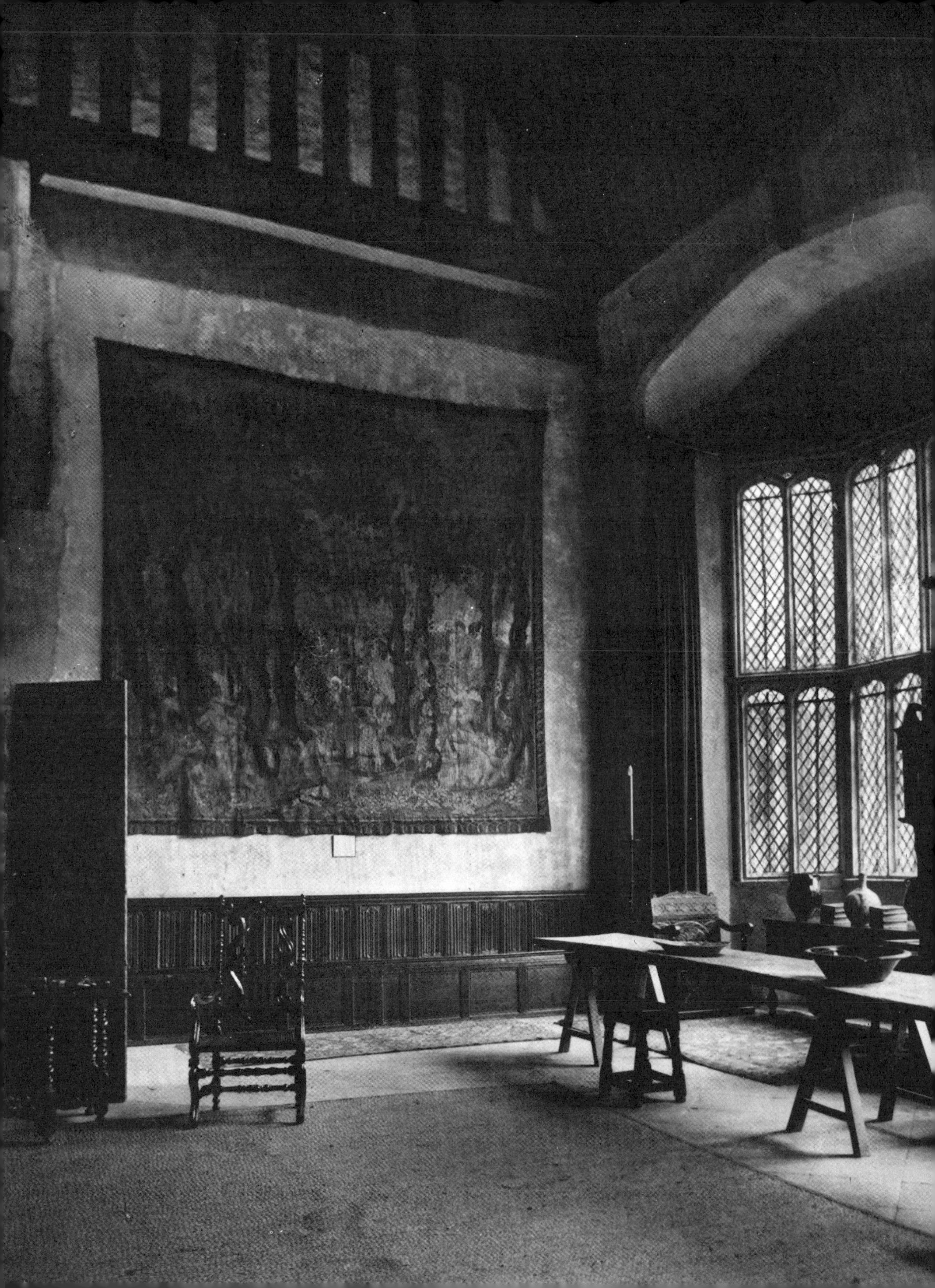

tection. The first great houses had been built on the castle plan, facing inwards onto a courtyard like Cowdray in Sussex. By Elizabeth's reign (1558–1603) they were looking outwards, built to impress the visitor with their Italian inspired classical symmetry. The Queen herself was often the visitor: the half-H or E plan allowed room for the long gallery and vast hall necessary for entertaining queen and court without the expense or stern exterior of the courtyard house. There was also room for a great chamber or parlour. Here the family could live a less communal life than had been possible in the great hall of the castle. Often, as at the Russell home, Chenies, there was also a smaller parlour or sitting room. Holdenby boasted "spacious chambers and withdrawing rooms" as well as "a beautiful gate house, magnificent towers and rare chimney pieces." Hatton told Burghley that the house put him £10,000 in debt. Burghley himself was surprisingly extravagant in his building. He had magnificent houses at Waltham and Cheshunt as well as Theobalds. He particularly loved his gardens. Laid out with arbors, knots, orchards, spinneys, walks, ponds and fountains, the sixteenth-century formal garden was an important part of the great house. Burghley employed forty men to look after the grounds at Theobalds.

Many of the new nobility adapted ecclesiastical buildings on their recently acquired monastic lands. Sir William Paulet turned Netley Abbey and Sir Edward Sharington converted Lacock Nunnery into comfortable homes. These were solid, undecorated buildings. Inside, the furnishings were almost as elaborate as those of the great prodigy houses. In his *Description of England* written early in Elizabeth's reign, the

A walled garden

Opposite The Great Hall of a Tudor house

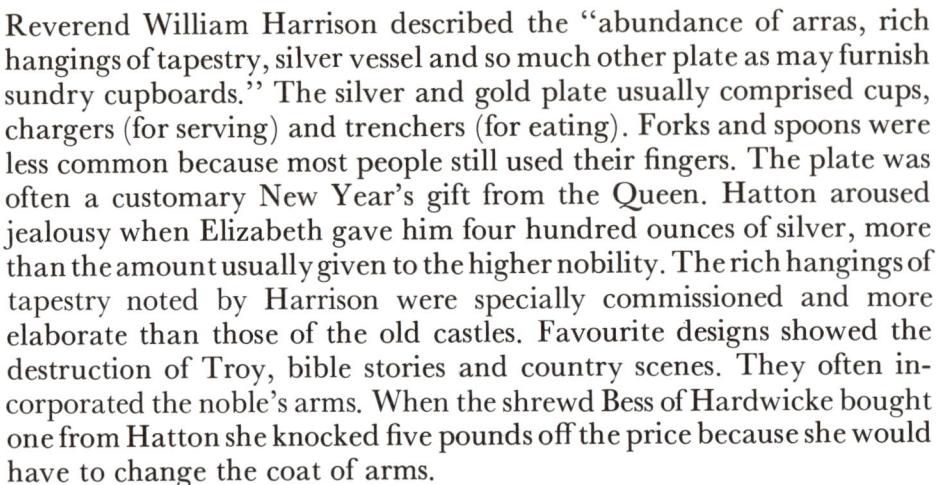

Reverend William Harrison described the "abundance of arras, rich hangings of tapestry, silver vessel and so much other plate as may furnish sundry cupboards." The silver and gold plate usually comprised cups, chargers (for serving) and trenchers (for eating). Forks and spoons were less common because most people still used their fingers. The plate was often a customary New Year's gift from the Queen. Hatton aroused jealousy when Elizabeth gave him four hundred ounces of silver, more than the amount usually given to the higher nobility. The rich hangings of tapestry noted by Harrison were specially commissioned and more elaborate than those of the old castles. Favourite designs showed the destruction of Troy, bible stories and country scenes. They often incorporated the noble's arms. When the shrewd Bess of Hardwicke bought one from Hatton she knocked five pounds off the price because she would have to change the coat of arms.

Elaborately carved fireplaces brought better insulation than the old open hearths: tapestries were still valued for their decoration but no longer required to keep out the draughts. By the end of the century they were being replaced by elaborate wainscotting or oak panelling. At Chenies, the Russells had tapestries in the hall and great parlour, panelling in the smaller sitting room. Ceilings no longer exposed beams and joists but were plastered over in complicated patterns. Floors, too were changing: rush matting gradually took the place of loose hay or rushes. Carpets were just coming in but were more often thrown over cupboards and tables than walked upon – they were too beautiful and expensive. Tables were now "joined" with hinged extensions instead of the old trestle type. The family needed a smaller table when they decided to eat alone. They still sat on wooden stools – now more comfortably shaped – for meals; but there was always at least one upholstered chair in each living room. The inventory for the small parlour at Chenies included "two drawinge joined tables of wallnot-tree," "turned stooles twentie" and "an old chaire of Tawney vellvette with tawneie silke fringe." Silk fringes also appeared in the bedrooms where the bed hangings and covers were luxuriously elaborate, often with the arms of the family embroidered on them in gold thread.

The Expenditure of the Tudor Nobility

Clothes, too, were heavily embroidered in silks and pearls. Lace and jewels weighed them down. Both sexes changed their silhouette because materials were so heavy. Hoops of wire called farthingales held out women's skirts. Men wore padded doublets; their waists were nipped in by decorated stomachers and their necks hidden by tall ruffs. The new fashions, the velvets and silks from Italy, also weighed heavily on aristocratic purses. William Shakespeare in *Henry VIII*, Part I, makes one duke comment to another that "many have broke their backs with Laying manors on 'em." The Earl of Leicester paid the equivalent of £543 for two cloaks and seven doublets embroidered with pearls.

To build and furnish a stately home, to clothe and feed his family and

Porcelain and silver goblet

Engraved glass bowl

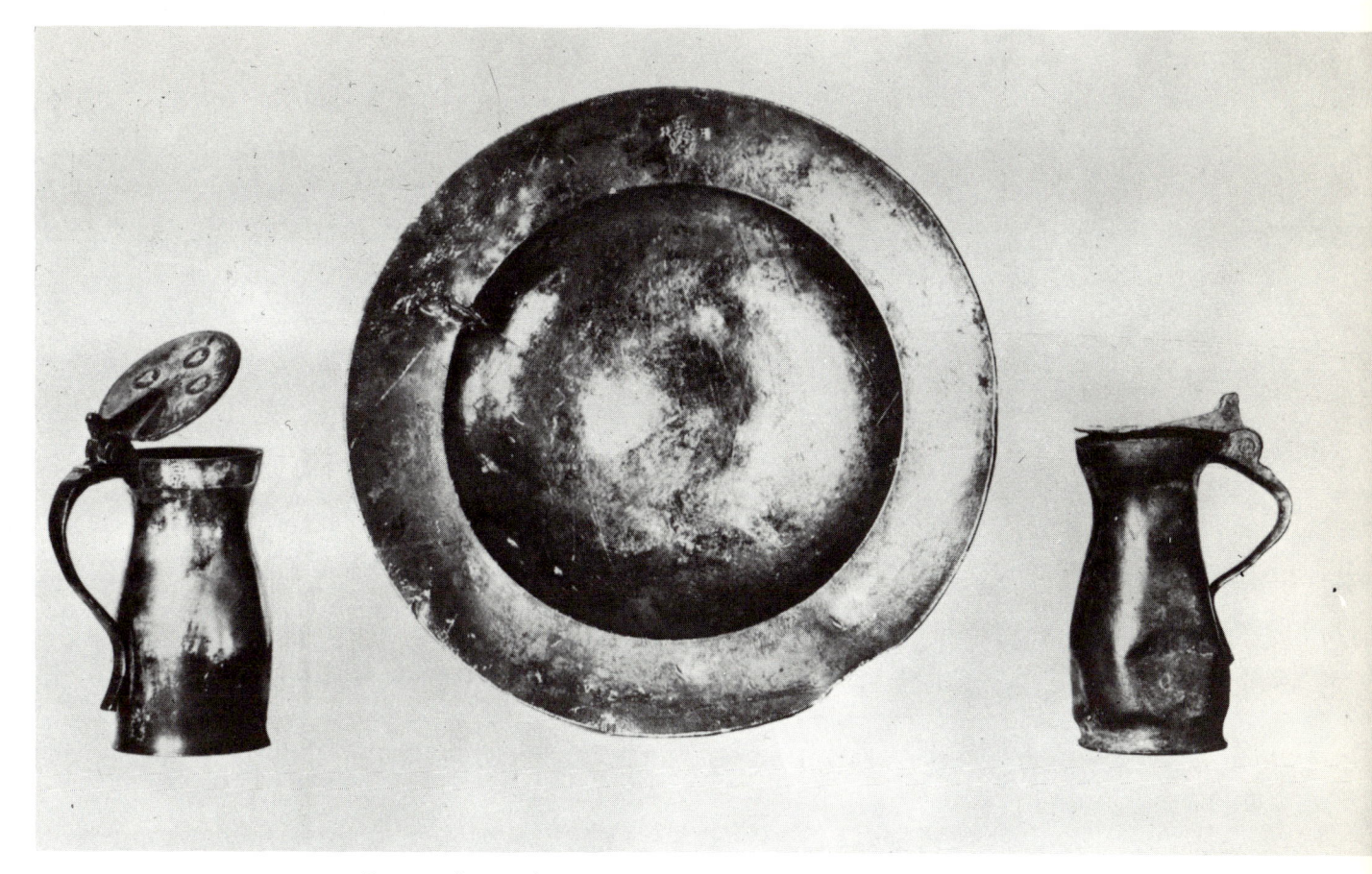

Pewter plate and mugs

household was enormously costly for the noble. The household accounts of the fifth Earl of Northumberland record an annual expenditure of £993 on his household of 166. (Figures must be multiplied by about 30 to reach the modern equivalent.) The Derby household accounts for 1561 show that the Earl spent £2,895 in one year. A large part went on food, including 56 oxen and 535 sheep.

Each child had his own mini-household. Each had to be educated as well as clothed, fed and waited upon. After his stay in another aristocratic household, the noble's son would expect to make the grand tour of Italy and France, spending some time at least in Venice, Naples and Paris. At the European courts he acquired a taste for extravagant clothes, furniture and architecture. Returning home, he would probably go to Oxford or Cambridge and then spend some time at the Inns of Court. Walsingham, Cecil and Bacon all went to Cambridge and Gray's Inn. This was considered a necessary prelude to public service even if a legal career was not envisaged. It was in any case a useful experience for the many law suits – themselves a continual expense – over property and feudal rights in which every landowner was periodically involved.

But the noble's expense did not end with his country and family responsibilities. His position demanded that he should also have a town

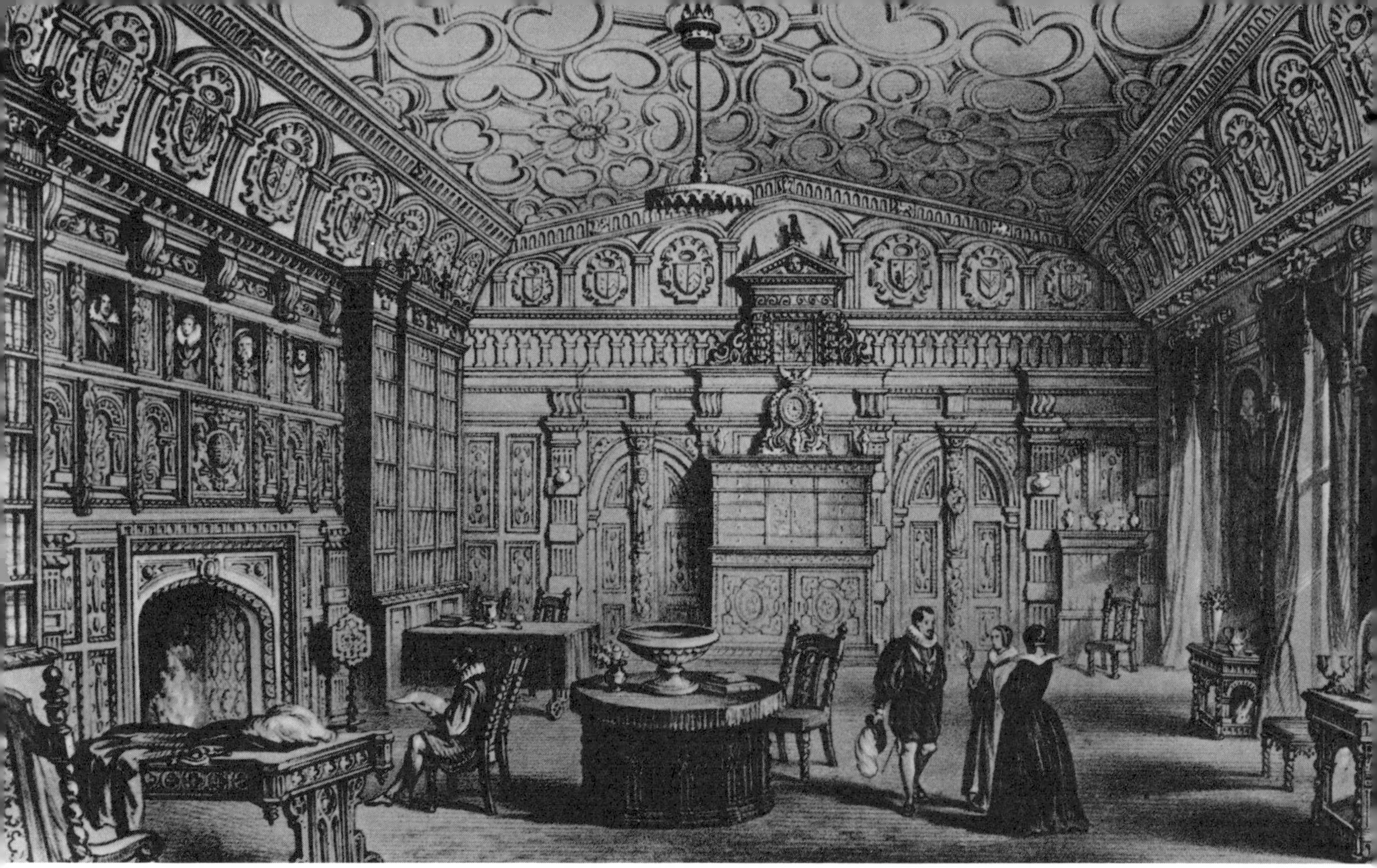

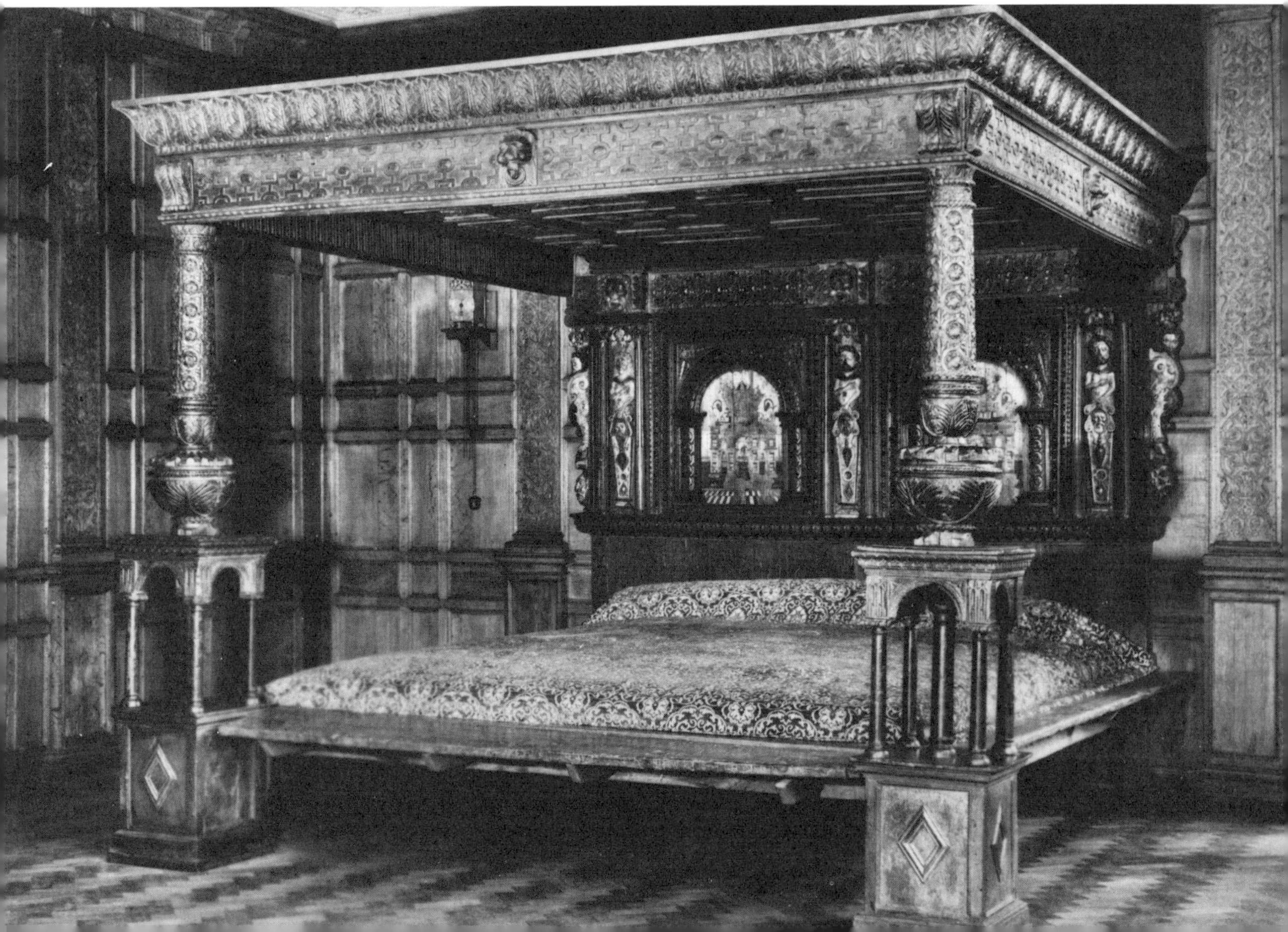

house. Hatton unscrupulously obtained the mansion of the Bishop of Ely in Holborn. The River Thames from Westminster to the City of London was lined with the mansions of the nobility, their gardens running down to the river. The households of Russell House, Somerset House and Essex House welcomed their earls when they came to London to take part in court life. And when the Queen went into the country to visit them, their expenses were even greater. While building Holdenby, Hatton swore he would not set eyes on his new house until "that holy saint" – meaning Elizabeth – "might sit in it." The Queen was only too eager to "sit" in her nobles' houses and save her own dwindling exchequer. With her she usually brought courtiers as well as the royal household. The Archbishop of Canterbury wrote to Burghley in 1573 before the Queen's visit to Canterbury that he had room for Sussex, Leicester, Hatton, Burghley himself and all their followers. The royal summer "progresses" were welcomed for their prestige, dreaded for their expense. Each time Burghley was host to Elizabeth he spent between £2,000 and £3,000. In 1575 Elizabeth's visit to Kenilworth cost Leicester £6,000. For her enjoyment he offered elaborate banquets and the currently popular masques and pageants. Other hosts might invite her to watch a tilting, a survival of the medieval tournament. Two horsemen met across a barrier or "tilt" and tried to hit each other with blunted spears. The armour worn for these occasions was elaborately decorated, designed for display rather than serious fighting. The Jacobe manuscript in the Victoria and Albert Museum contains illustrations of the suits worn by Hatton, Leicester and others and probably made by Jacob Halder, the Master Armourer at Greenwich under Elizabeth.

The nobility were generous in entertaining the Queen, each other and strangers. An Italian visitor remarked: "They would sooner give five or six ducats to provide an entertainment for a person than a groat [low value coin] to assist him in any distress." They were often asked to play host to visiting ambassadors. Elizabeth also expected them to act as ambassadors abroad for her. This in itself was a great expense for them and an honour they did their best to avoid. The Earl of Bedford was only just persuaded to represent Elizabeth in France at the accession of Charles IX in 1561: it was pointed out to him that, as the French court was in mourning, his followers would not need sumptuous liveries. The Earl of Northumberland pleaded deafness to excuse him from a visit abroad. Leicester's command in the Netherlands forced him to borrow from Palavicino and left him £70,000 in debt. At home, too, offices under the crown could bring debt rather than profit. The Earl of Huntingdon ran up £20,000 in debts during his twenty years as Lord President of the North.

Many nobles complained of their heavy expenses and their debts. Henry Percy, the ninth earl, told his son: "I came to be an erle of Northumberland so well left for moveables as I was not worth a fyershovell or a paire of tongs." Some, like Leicester, pawned plate and jewels; others, like the Earl of Norfolk, mortgaged some of their lands. These cases have been built up by some historians into a picture of an

Opposite top A library in a Tudor aristocrat's home
Opposite bottom A huge, ornate sixteenth century bed

Tudor aristocratic fashion

48

c

A young nobleman

A kitchen in a sixteenth century aristocrat's household

aristocracy impoverished by their inability to cope with changing economic conditions. According to Professor R. H. Tawney and his disciples, the old nobility were slower than the new gentry, with their financial and business expertise, to enclose land, raise rents and evict tenants in answer to the rise in prices. But many of the old, and certainly the new, nobility were quite as efficient in this respect as the gentry. Those in debt suffered more from their heavy expenses than any inability to run their estates. Moreover, while they had their vast estates the nobles were hardly poverty stricken. The very size of their debts proves their credit worthiness. Very few were so impoverished that their loss of land deprived them also of the right to be summoned to the Lords and thus their titles. The exceptions were families like the De Veres, earls of Oxford, who were already poorly endowed with lands and had particularly dissolute heirs.

It was not the royal policy to make the old aristocracy bankrupt. Otherwise Elizabeth would not have granted them valuable patents and wardships as well as land. The Earl of Warwick received a twelve-year monopoly of trade to Barbary and the wardship of the young Earl of Bedford, worth £609 a year. The Queen in fact helped to maintain many noble families, acting always through Lord Burghley. A contemporary wrote that "by occasion of his office he hath preserved many great houses from overthrow by relieving sundry extremities." So long as they were no longer powerful rivals, Elizabeth wanted the support of the

Young nobles receiving their education

The River Thames, London, lined with mansions

51

Queen Elizabeth visiting Kenilworth Castle, home of the Earl of Leicester

A hunting picnic for Elizabeth I. The aristocracy were expected to entertain the Queen on a lavish scale

nobility, not its destruction. By making them attend her as courtiers she made sure that their influence in the country diminished. At court they came into contact with dramatists and painters. They established the idea of patronage of the artist by the aristocracy which was to continue for two centuries. Sir Christopher Hatton's protégés included the musician William Byrd, the alchemist Dr. John Dee and the painter Cornelius Ketel. The poet Edmund Spenser wrote a sonnet to him. The Earl of Northumberland gave pensions to mathematicians and geographers. In a less happy period of his life he found enough cultural interest among the nobles imprisoned in the Tower with him to form a Literary and Philosophical Society.

Elizabeth's reluctance to grant new titles was itself due to her wish to preserve the old aristocracy as a social elite. The families of her new administrators often had to acquire lands and prove their loyalty in service to the crown before they or their heirs could join that elite. The old aristocracy had the titles; the new men the power. By depriving the former of influence and making the latter work hard for their honours, Elizabeth made sure that the whole nobility was dependent on her. In one century the nobility had become a support instead of a rival to the crown.

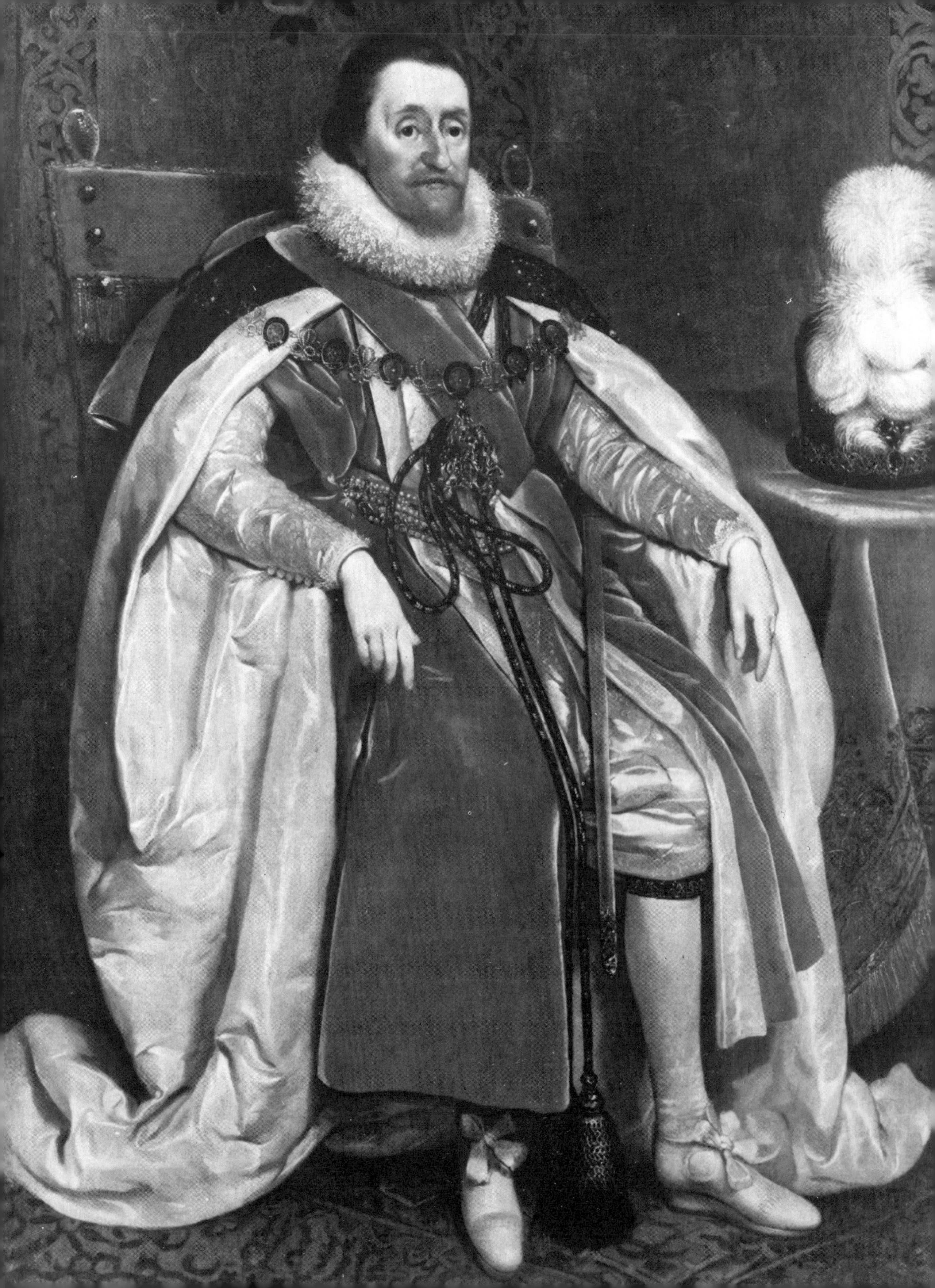

4 Outliving the Kings

James I and the Creation of New Peers

JAMES I was welcomed to the throne in 1603 by clamourings from Elizabeth's loyal servants. They demanded that their frustrated hopes for titles should be satisfied. James made Sir Robert Cecil first a baron, then a viscount, then Earl of Salisbury. Sir Robert Sidney became Earl of Leicester. Sir Francis Bacon, grandson of a sheepreeve (manager of an estate's sheep flock) and son of Elizabeth's Keeper of the Court of Wards who had bought thirty manors, was created Viscount St. Albans.

James also restored several old titles: the Earldom of Essex went back to Robert Devereux whose father had been executed. Members of the Howard family who had plotted with Mary Queen of Scots and Philip II of Spain against the throne were honoured with the Earldoms of Suffolk and Arundel. None were resented: land and birth were accepted as justifiable criteria for ennoblement. But merit alone was not considered enough. There was an outcry when James made Lionel Cranfield the Earl of Middlesex. Cranfield had served James well in the Court of Wards, the navy and the Treasury, introducing reforms and savings; but he was still only a landless London merchant.

By the end of the reign (1625) the number of British peers had risen from 55 to 121. Some were James's favourites: Robert Carr became Earl of Somerset and George Villiers, Duke of Buckingham. Charles II (1660–85) swelled the ranks further. Edward Hyde was given the Earldom of Clarendon. His successors and those of the five members of Charles' Cabal (his secret cabinet of ministers) who were also made earls are still represented in today's peerage. While Charles' ministers won earldoms, his illegitimate sons were considered worthy of dukedoms. Lucy Walter's son became the Duke of Monmouth; Barbara Palmer provided the nation with the Dukes of Southampton, Grafton and Somerset; Nell Gwyn the Duke of St. Albans, Louise de Kerouillac the Duke of Richmond.

But most of James I's new titles were neither rewards nor favours. They were commodities sold for profit. After his break with Parliament in 1615, James was faced with the need for money as well as with the continual demand for honours. He neatly answered both problems by selling titles to the highest bidders. He even created a whole new order, the baronetcy, with a fixed price of £1,000 for a new title. Sales paid for the colonization of Ulster. Charles I copied his father's method when he

Opposite James I (1603–1625)

55

Francis Bacon, later Viscount St. Albans

colonized Nova Scotia.

John Pym complained in Parliament that men were ennobled according to the heaviness of their purse rather than for the weightiness of their merit. The Duke of Buckingham was in charge of most transactions. At his impeachment by the Commons in 1626 he was accused of ennobling his own family and indulging in the peerage traffic for his own profit: "Whereas the titles of honour of this kingdom of England were wont to be conferred as great rewards, upon such virtuous and industrious persons as had merited them by their faithful service, the said Duke by his importunate and subtile procurements, hath perverted that ancient and honourable way..."

James's policies were short sighted; they were continued by Charles after 1625. Title-selling swelled the resentment against the crown which cost him his head. As he needed more money for his struggle against the Parliamentarians Charles was forced to continue the unpopular methods. As late as September, 1648, when he was a prisoner at Carisbrooke, he wrote to Brudenell, asking for £1,000 with which to bribe his gaolers and pay his supporters: "Your doing this courtesy for me... I do hereby promise you, as soon as I have a great seal in my power, to confer upon you the title and honour of an earl of this kingdom." Brudenell managed to raise the money. He was duly rewarded after the restoration of 1660 with the Earldom of Cardigan.

Decline in Respect for the Nobility

The status of the aristocracy suffered from the sale of titles. Elizabeth I may have undermined the real power of the nobility, but it had remained a respected elite. At the beginning of the seventeenth century it was felt by contemporary writers, even republicans, to have an important place in the constitution and in society. Fulke Greville (1554–1628), poet and courtier, thought the aristocracy filled a useful role as "brave halfe paces between a Throne and a People;" Henry Neville wrote: "Though their dependences and power are gone, yet we cannot be without them."

But respect for the nobility declined as Buckingham added his relatives, hangers-on and subscribers to it. The creation of so many new titles would have threatened the prestige of the existing elite even if they had been given to men of merit. But now the quality as well as the quantity of the new peers lowered the whole nobility in the esteem of the rest of the country. Several cases were reported of nobles complaining of arrogant treatment by the gentry class. For example, Thomas Bennett dared to argue with the Earl of Marlborough over a hunting dispute.

The relationship between landlord and tenant was now an economic rather than a personal one. A few peers, like the Stanleys in Lincolnshire, played a prominent part in country life under the Stuarts. Most of them, even though they might be lord lieutenants of their county, delegated their duties to deputies while they remained at court. These duties were in any case becoming fewer. Local administration was being carried out

Edward Hyde, Earl of Clarendon

Opposite top George Villiers, Duke of Buckingham (with family)
Opposite bottom Revelries in a noble household, early seventeenth century

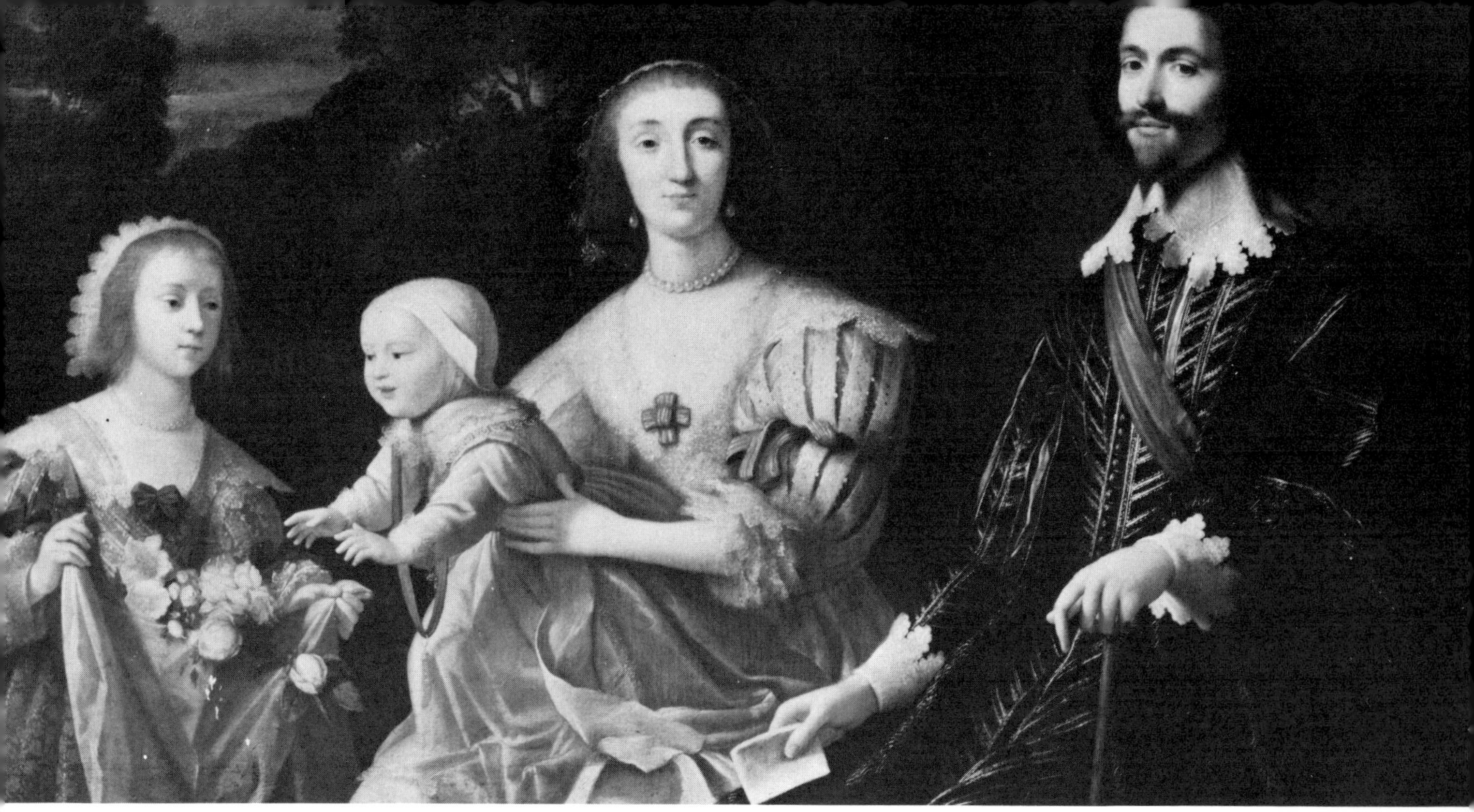

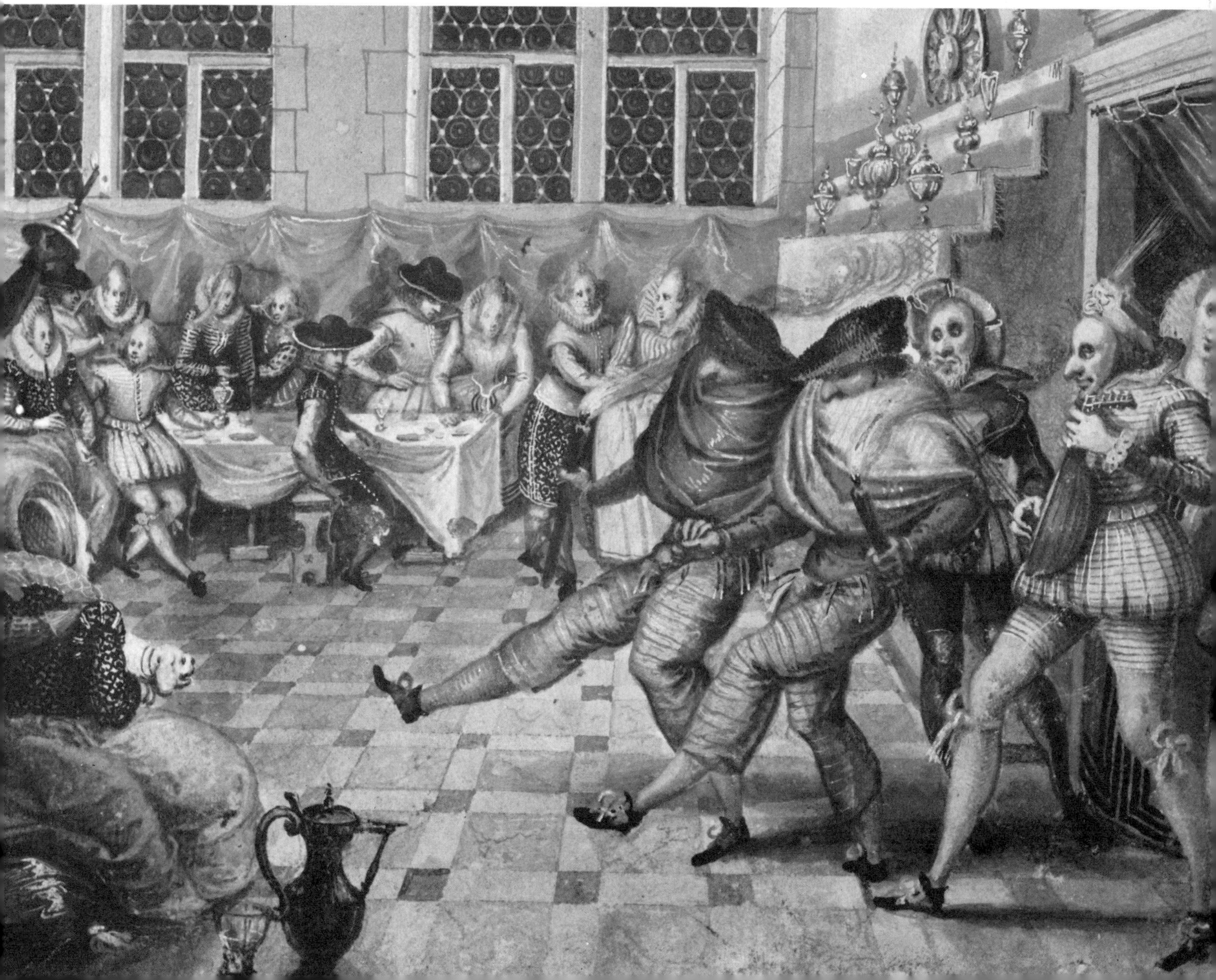

Nell Gwyn. Her illegitimate son by Charles II was made Duke of St. Albans

more and more by agents of the central government with the help of the local gentry. There was little grassroots contact with the peers in the counties. Moreover, fewer noble families than before owned many manors in their own counties. With less influence they could no longer count on the habit of subservient obedience to the lord of the manor. Hierarchical attitudes and cap doffing were going out of fashion.

Puritan belief in the importance of the private conscience began to influence general attitudes towards the secular hierarchy. It also promoted distaste for the behaviour of the peers at court. The playwrights satirized the nobility. John Marston made Malevole claim in his play *The Malcontent* (1604): "I am of noble kind, for I find myself possessed with all their qualities: love dogs, dice and drabs; have beat my shoemaker, knocked my seamstress, cuckold my 'pothecary, and undone my tailor." Too many of the newly ennobled had too little to do.

Opposite top A medieval noblewoman goes hunting

Opposite bottom Dinner at the home of a lord. Middle Ages

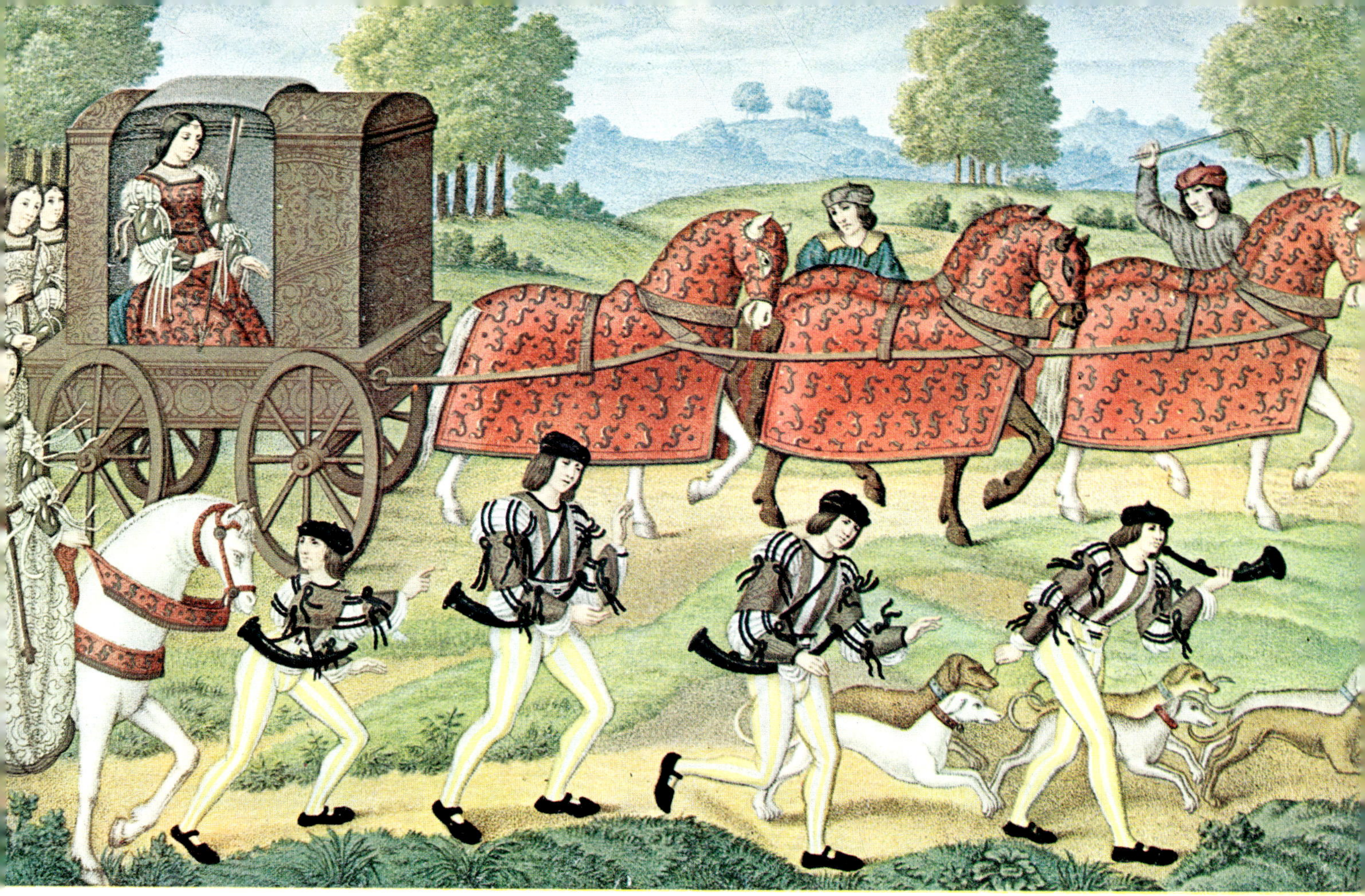

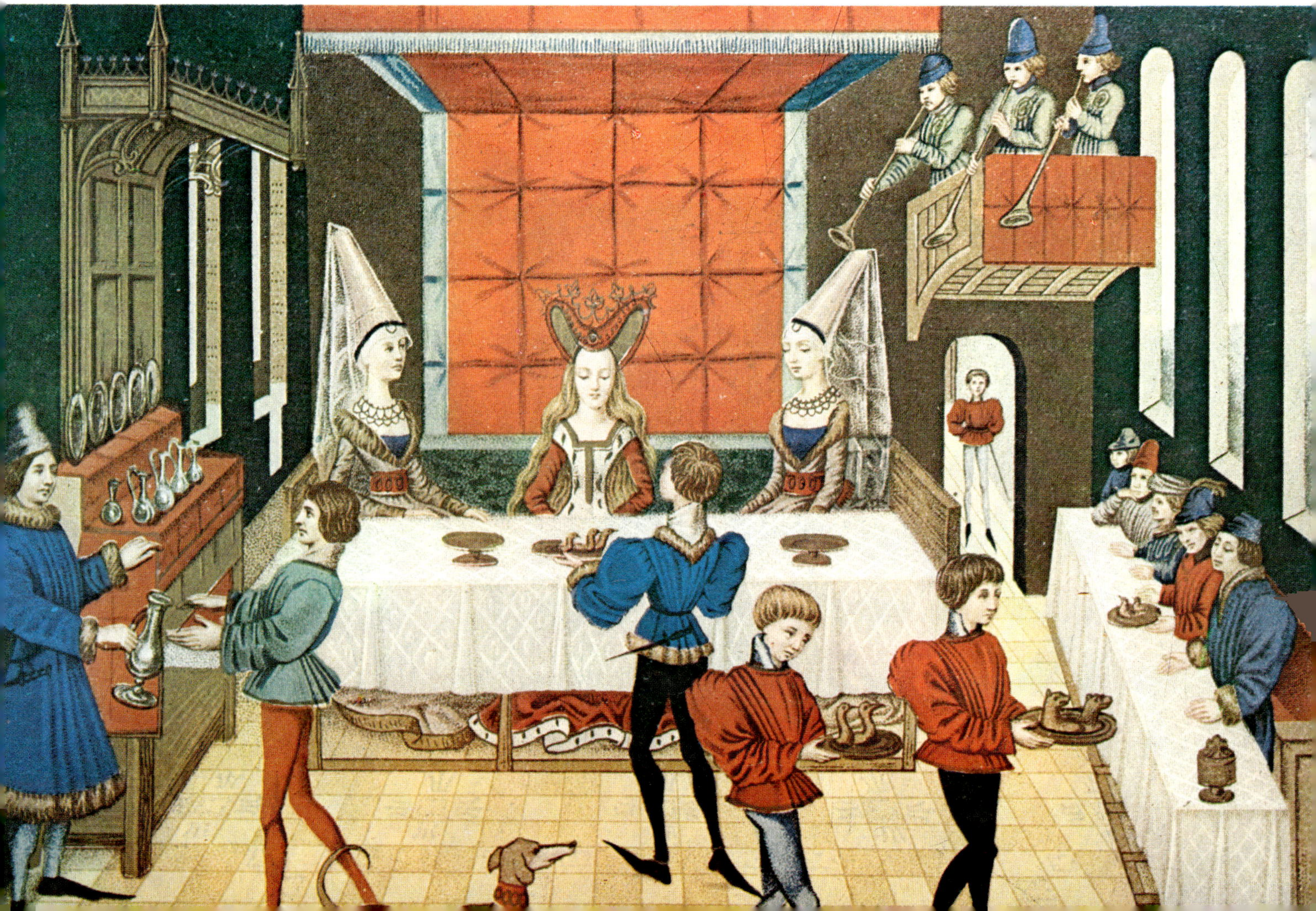

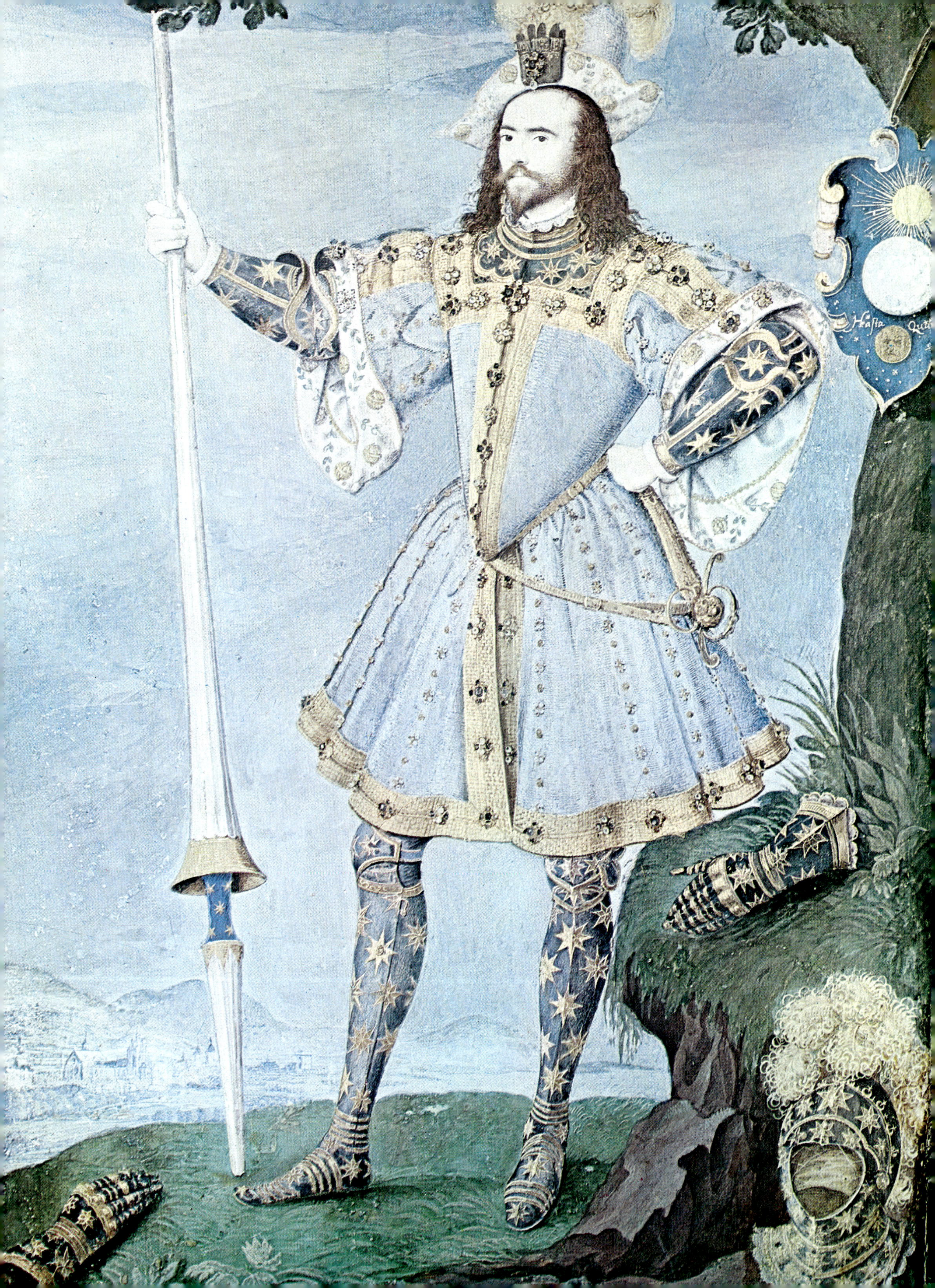
Hasta

Bottom Lord Squander arranges a marriage of convenience (his son and future daughter in law are at the left of the picture) A satirical painting by Hogarth

Top Noblemen hunting near Nonesuch Palace, sixteenth century

Opposite George Clifford, third Duke of Cumberland (1558–1605)

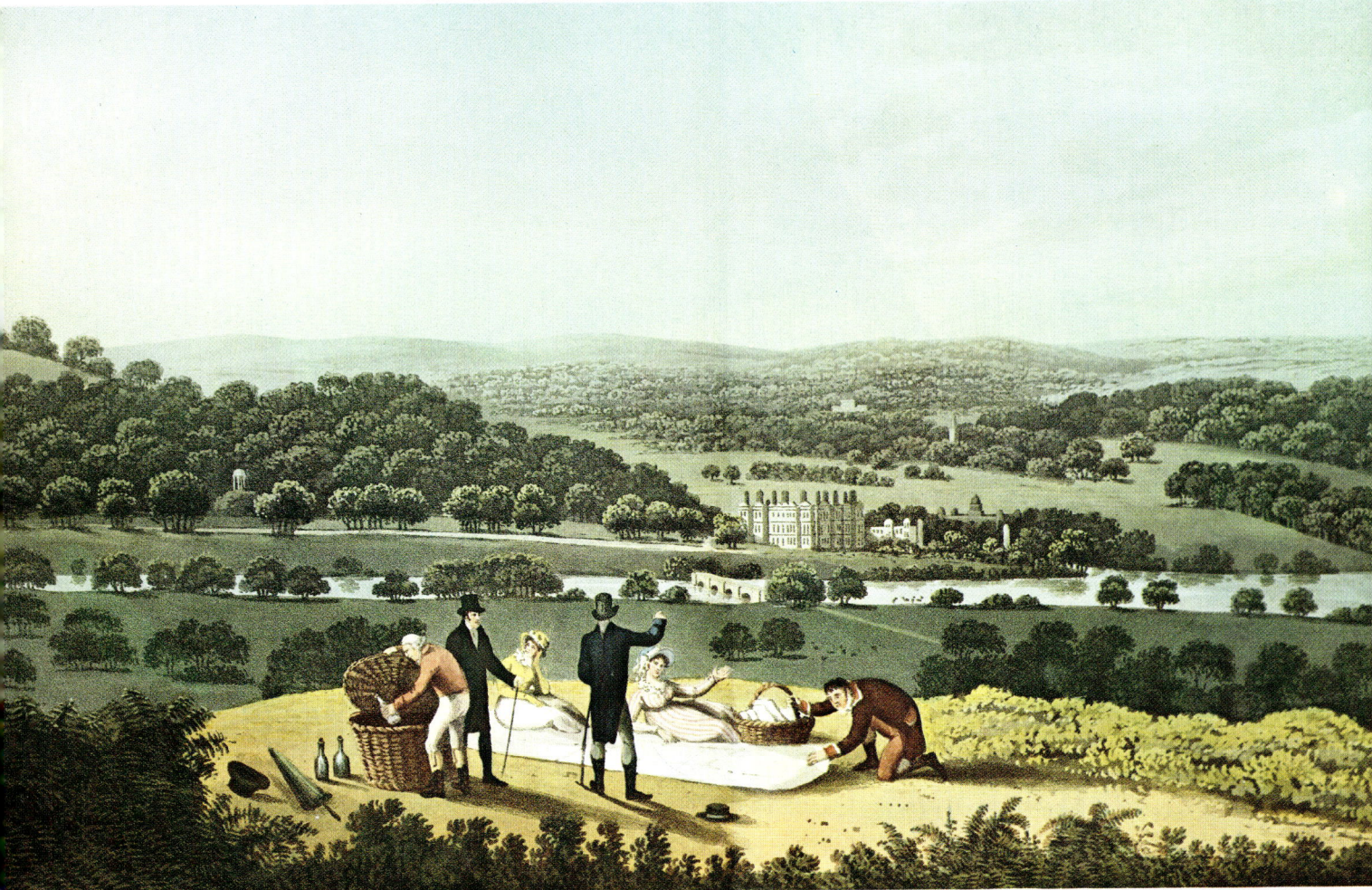

Lord Althorp and friends take tea. Eighteenth century

A view of Longleat, home of the Marquess of Bath. Early nineteenth century

There were not enough offices at court to satisfy more than a few. They spent much time drinking, gambling, watching plays and exchanging mistresses. Those who came back to Charles II's court at the Restoration (1660) took up these pursuits with renewed enthusiasm. Many had spent their youth abroad during the interregnum with no occupation, or had been demoralized by the uncertainties of the Civil War. One of their leaders was Thomas, later Lord, Wharton. He was well known for writing songs about Charles bringing over Irish Catholics to cut English Protestant throats and for urinating on a church altar while drunk. The Duke's Theatre was the favourite haunt of the young nobles, one of whom introduced Charles to Nell Gwyn there after her performance.

Charles II (1660–1685)

64

The plays performed there reflected their tastes: William Wycherley's *The Country Wife*, then later Vanbrugh's *The Relapse* and William Congreve's *Love for Love* wittily depicted the sexual morality of the court. Political morals, too, had lapsed since the departure of the upright Burghley. The Earl of Shaftesbury for instance, was quite willing to support Titus Oates in his perpetration of the myth of a Jesuit conspiracy in an effort to topple the throne of James II (1685–88).

There was one very practical reason for the decline of aristocratic power and prestige: the nobility were no longer a military elite. Under the Tudors their castles had become country mansions and their armed followers household retainers; but most of them had gained military experience in the Wars of the Roses. Now, even their household retainers were cut down. By the beginning of the seventeenth century only one peer in five had ever actually fought in a battle. The art of warfare demanded expertise in engineering, transport and administration. It was a matter for the trained band rather than the local lord. The eighty peers who fought for the crown were no match for Oliver Cromwell's New Model Army. The aristocracy had lost military superiority as surely as local influence. Moreover, involvement in rebellion against the monarch was becoming disreputable. Propaganda from pulpit and press preached loyalty to the king as a religious and national virtue. Parliament had taken the place of the nobility as the rival to the crown.

Opposite Fashions reflected the great wealth of the Stuart aristocracy

Economic Status of the Stuart Nobility

While the power and prestige of the aristocracy waned, its prosperity actually grew. As a result of his research in the 1940s Professor R. H. Tawney concluded that the economic position of the peerage had declined in relation to the rest of the landed gentry before and after the Civil War. But recent research has not borne this out. The nobility certainly did not suffer unduly from the Civil War itself. The conflict was political and religious, not social. There was no animosity towards the aristocracy as such. Only the small sect of "Diggers" actually demanded a redistribution of land and they were quickly destroyed by the army. Some church and crown lands were sold to Cromwell's soldier and merchant followers. But they made no attempt to set themselves up as country gentlemen. At the Restoration there was no sign of any new aristocracy to rival the position of the old.

Very few estates of the royalist nobles were confiscated. After the Earl of Bedford had changed his allegiance from Parliament to Charles, two parliamentary commissioners arrived at Bedford House. They seized furniture and tapestries but did not lay any claim to the Russells' urban or country estates. Those whose property had been confiscated were able to redeem it under the Commonwealth with fines equivalent to two years rent or a tenth of the total value, whichever was the greater. Such was the wealth of the great landowners that these payments were usually managed without undue hardship. It was the upper gentry or untitled aristocracy like the Penruddock family who suffered casualties

A cavalryman in Oliver Cromwell's New Model Army. Trained soldiers had replaced armies supplied by local lords

65

E

through their more intense involvement in the war and financial hardship because they were less able to pay heavy fines.

Professor Stone has pointed out the dangers of "counting manors" to show the decline in aristocratic wealth: some manors were worth far more than others; and other factors compensated individual noble families for decreased acreage. It may be true that only six noble families owned more than seventy manors in 1641 as compared with eighteen in 1559. But these figures are significant for the territorial influence, not the real incomes of the aristocracy. During the first half of the seventeenth century there was a desperate demand for land by private buyers because of a rise in population thirty years earlier. This demand depleted noble estates; but it also sent land values and rents soaring, to the advantage of the nobility.

Receipts from land were further increased by an improvement in agricultural methods and technology. The accounts of the Russell family give us an insight into the way in which the fortunes of a typical noble family were boosted. The fourth Earl's careful and progressive management increased the income from the estates at Tavistock and Woburn. The family also owned land in swampy Cambridgeshire. When the first earl had received the grant of the dissolved abbey at Thorney he had considered it valueless. But Francis Russell, the fourth earl, introduced a successful drainage scheme. The fens became good agricultural and hunting land, supplying the family at Woburn and London with valuable produce as well as rents. Receipts from Thorney rose from £1,000 in 1641 to £5,000 in 1662. The Earls of Rutland and Shrewsbury also extracted maximum value from their land: their forests fired the furnaces which produced iron, lead and steel for sale to London merchants. The Duke of Montagu had an iron works on his Beaulieu estate. Technical and industrial enterprise were not yet the prerogatives of the middle class.

Incomes rose from urban as well as country properties. Both prospering gentry and newly rich merchants wanted town houses. Rents from the Russells' Covent Garden property became a valuable asset. The third earl had considered selling it to pay off his debts in 1601. Luckily he was prevented from doing so. The fourth earl employed Inigo Jones to build elegant houses and St. Paul's church in a beautifully proportioned square behind Bedford House in the Strand. During the late 1640s and 1650s the Piazza became a fashionable residential area and rents rose accordingly. The Russells' tenants in the square included the Marquess of Winchester, the Earl of Sussex, the Countess of Peterborough, Sir Harry Vane and several baronets. In 1671 the fifth earl was granted the royal patent to hold a market "within the Piazza of Covent Garden." The total annual income from the Russells' country and urban estates was far greater in 1640 than 1602; and increased from £8,500 in 1640 to £14,000 in the 1670s (about £560,000 today). Such profits enabled the great landowners to take in their stride the slump in wool prices in 1620 and the heavy land taxes after 1642. It was the smaller landlords who suffered from them.

The rising income from land would itself have ensured aristocratic prosperity. But the nobility had other sources of income. Some invested their riches in shipping and stock companies. Others lent money at the six per cent rate made statutory in 1651. The Marquess of Carmarthen persuaded Peter the Great to grant him the concession of importing Virginia tobacco into Russia.

The tolerance towards trade enabled many aristocratic families to build their fortunes through marriage. Robert Cecil, influenced by Elizabeth's snobbish desire to keep the nobility a closed elite, had been disgusted when the daughter of Lord Howard of Bindon had married an alderman. But the seventeenth-century peers, many of whom had after all bought their titles, were less hierarchical in their attitude. Lord Compton won a reprieve from debt by marrying the daughter of Sir John "Rich" Spencer, a wealthy merchant and one time Lord Mayor of London. In the 1620s there were several marriage alliances between peers and the widows or daughters of city merchants. James Shirley the playwright commented in 1628 that there was

"not a virgin
Left by her friends heir to a noble fortune
But she's in danger of a marriage
To some puff'd title."

Marriages within the aristocracy were more important in consolidating the greater landed fortunes. Heiresses were much sought after. William Russell added Bloomsbury to the Bedford estates by his marriage to Rachel Wriothesley, the co-heiress of the Earl of Southampton. Rachel's sister married into the Montagu family, taking the Beaulieu estate with her.

Lucrative royal offices and favours – sinecures, pensions and monopolies – swelled the incomes of the nobles at court. The Earl of Bridgwater is said to have made more than £700,000 out of his appointment as Paymaster to Marlborough's army. Professor Stone estimates that such favours provided as much as a quarter of the total assets of the aristocracy in 1641. The distinction grew between those courtier nobles dependent more and more on royal favours for their prosperity, and those who preferred to spend their time improving their estates. They were called the town and country parties; otherwise known by the pejorative terms of Tories and Whigs.

The nobility led a luxurious life on their increased incomes. They were certainly suffering no economic decline. The ruin of the Earl of Cleveland after extravagant spending was exceptional. Most could afford huge wardrobes. The Stuarts themselves led the fashion for rich clothes with elaborate trimmings. James I, over a period of five years, bought a new cloak every month, a waistcoat every three weeks, a suit every ten days, stockings and boots every five days and new gloves every day. His courtiers naturally copied his example; the new fashions then spread to the city and the country house. The Duke of Buckingham estimated the

Lady riding side saddle. A half skirt (safeguard) protects her from mud

Seventeenth century banquet

Jacobean interior. There were more small rooms in large seventeenth century houses

cost of his clothes in 1627 at £3,000. Exotic feathers for noble hats, gold buttons, embroidery in pearls and gold thread all added to the expense. At a court banquet in 1613 Margaret Lady Wotton arrived in a gown whose embroidery alone cost £50 a yard; Viscount Montagu's daughters' dresses set him back £1,500.

At such a banquet the food was as extravagant as the clothes of the guests. Lord Hay, future Earl of Carlisle, fed the French ambassador and his other guests at Essex House in 1621 on 12 six-foot Russian salmon, 12 pheasants, 24 partridges, 144 larks, two swans and two pigs at a cost of over £3,000. This was hardly an everyday meal; but vast quantities of meat, never cheap, were consumed in aristocratic households. In a typical week the Earl of Shrewsbury's family and servants ate 23 sheep, two bullocks, one cow, 59 chickens, 5 pigs, 24 pigeons and 54 rabbits. Good wine was appreciated as much as good food. During the century port, "Shampagne" – which figures in the Russell accounts for the first time in 1665 – and later brandy were added to aristocratic cellars. Coffee in the 1670s and tea in the 1680s were also becoming popular.

The family now ate, except on festive occasions, in a small dining room. This was a feature of all the great houses built at this time. Like the corridors which did away with the necessity of having one room lead out of another, it was a sign of the family's growing desire for a private life. At Woburn, built by Inigo Jones for the fourth Earl of Bedford, the dining parlour opened off the great hall in the west wing. It was balanced on the other side by a small sitting room; behind the entrance hall was a grotto open to the garden. Above were the state rooms for banquets. The family lived in the north wing – the Italian influence still demanding that the most frequented rooms should receive no sunlight. This plan, designed around the courtyard, was typical of most aristocratic houses. The Earl of Salisbury's Hatfield House – built on the site of an old palace James I had persuaded Cecil to exchange for Theobalds – was more ornate with elaborate towers, gateways and columns. He spent £40,000 and four years building it. This was swift compared with the eighteen years taken by the Duke of Devonshire to complete Chatsworth.

Apart from Hatfield, Salisbury built Cranborne in Dorset, a house in Chelsea, and Salisbury House in the Strand. Every peer had his town

Seventeenth century coach

Sedan chair

Hatfield House, home of the Earl of Salisbury

houses; most had more than one country estate. Travelling between their great houses was not cheap, involving overnight stops, horses and at least one coach worth about £50. In town a nobleman needed a prestige coach with six horses, silk upholstery and decorative gilding. The Duke of Rutland in 1623 paid his coach builder £60, his silkman £71 and his gilder £42. The Earl of Bedford's new coach, ordered for Charles II's coronation but delivered too late, boasted the newest feature of glass instead of leather flaps in the windows and cost £170. After the Restoration a law was passed to limit the amount of gilding on coaches in order to prevent the waste of gold. Few nobles took any notice of it. They might also spend £25 on a sedan chair, popular in the 1630s, for private visits in town. The sedan was as hated as the new hackney carriages by the Thames watermen who now lost their livelihood, as people became less dependent on river transport.

Most of the noble's travelling was done between his own great houses. He might sometimes visit other aristocratic mansions or take a trip to one of the newly fashionable spas. The fifth Earl of Bedford regularly took the waters at Bath for his gout and rheumatism. Queen Henrietta Maria, wife of Charles I, patronized Tunbridge Wells. Before the Civil War the Belgian spas had been more in favour; but the inconvenience of crossing the Channel had ensured the success of the new English resorts.

The British aristocracy did not like to leave their country estates or court for foreign travel. But they sent their sons abroad. The "grand tour" of France and Italy was now an accepted part of the education of a nobleman's son. It usually followed private tuition by a tutor and a spell at Oxford or Cambridge. A special travelling tutor was hired to accompany the young lord on his travels. The Earl of Bedford's two middle sons were away for an extended tour of six years with their tutor, Charles Rich. They stayed in Paris, Saumur, Rome, Venice, Florence, Bologna and Brussels, attending universities and seminaries and sending home Italian lace and glass to add to the splendours of Woburn and Bedford House.

The private tutor in the aristocratic home was in some cases now replaced by boarding school. While the Earl of Bedford's four elder sons were taught by John Thornton at Woburn, the two youngest were sent at eight to a private school at Twickenham and then to Westminster. The other most popular school among the nobility was Eton. In the early 1630s it was attended by the sons of the Earls of Peterborough, Dover, Cork, Southampton and Northumberland. The popularity of the boarding school affected the daughters as well as the sons of the aristocracy. Previously they had shared their brothers' tutors; now they were handed over to the governess and their education followed a different pattern.

The demands of their children's education, their libraries and their private portrait galleries – artists like Peter Lely and Van Dyke were in demand to immortalize the aristocrat and his family – meant that the nobility was now indulging in heavy spending the results of which were not particularly conspicuous. It was no longer necessary either to die or

Opposite top Bath, a spa favoured by the aristocracy
Opposite bottom Eton, a popular school of the aristocracy

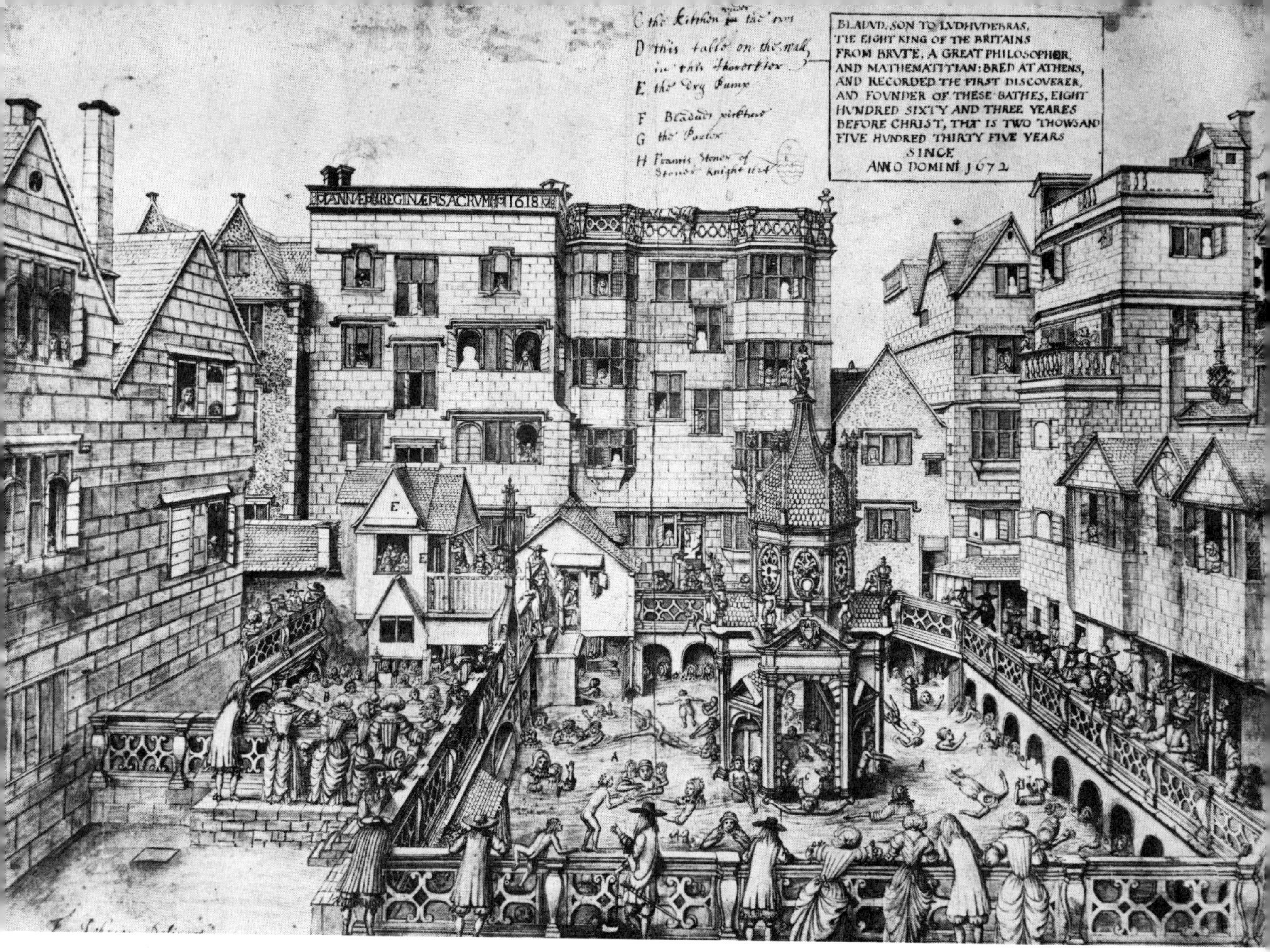
BLADVD, SON TO LVDHVDEBRAS,
THE EIGHT KING OF THE BRITAINS
FROM BRVTE, A GREAT PHILOSOPHER,
AND MATHEMATITIAN: BRED AT ATHENS,
AND RECORDED THE FIRST DISCOVERER,
AND FOVNDER OF THESE BATHES, EIGHT
HVNDRED SIXTY AND THREE YEARES
BEFORE CHRIST, THAT IS TWO THOWSAND
FIVE HVNDRED THIRTY FIVE YEARS
SINCE
ANNO DOMINI 1672

be buried with public ostentation. A contemporary wrote in 1631 that "Funerals in any expensive way here with us are now accounted but a fruitlesse vanitie, for we see daily that noblemen are either silently buried in the night time, with a torch and a lanterne or parsimoniously interred in the daytime by the helpe of some ignorant countrey-painter."

A funeral now meant family mourning, not a chance to show off its riches. In many cases their growing concern with their families and estates made the nobility less interested in communal or national affairs. The fourth Earl of Bedford resented the time he had to spend in London attending the King's Council. His son became General of the Horse for the Parliamentary side in the summer of 1642 but had resigned before the end of the year. As the Countess of Dorset remarked, the Russells disapproved at once of the character of the Stuarts and the politics of Cromwell. This attitude was typical of the twenty peers who remained neutral during the Civil War, and also of many who thought it best to support one side or the other. Frustration among the courtiers in their attempts to gain profitable office meant that even many of Charles I's aristocratic supporters were lukewarm in their support as well as militarily incompetent. Unlike the fifteenth- or eighteenth-century noble, the seventeenth-century aristocrat was not a political animal.

The noble's obsession was with his land and with the improvement and consolidation of his estates. His prosperity grew year by year after the Restoration of 1660. If, like the Russells, his estates dated from Reformation grants (and the Dissolution of the monasteries), he was only too glad to put an end to the Catholic threat of James II and the fear that the church might reclaim its land; he therefore supported the Protestant William of Orange. The events of 1688, when William was offered the English throne, far from being revolutionary, upheld the rights of property. William gave his Dutch favourites, Van Keppel and Bentinck, estates in his new country and transformed them into British aristocrats, the Earls of Albemarle and Portland. They joined the existing earls, marquesses and dukes whose estates were becoming more and more profitable. A distinct rift was opening between these great landowners, the upper aristocracy, and the less prosperous viscounts and barons. The scene was set for the rule of the eighteenth-century oligarchy.

5 The Whig Oligarchy

Between 1690 and 1790 English political and social life was dominated by a small coterie of 150 aristocrats. Between them they owned nearly one-fifth of cultivated England and Wales. Whatever their talents, interests and activities, it was their acres that made them the strongest aristocratic oligarchy since the Normans.

Wealth and the Eighteenth Century Aristocracy

The growing obsession with property had not only helped to ensure William of Orange's victory over James II in 1688; it had created a prejudice against the splitting up of aristocratic estates by sales or bequests. Stricter laws governed the disposal of land; primogeniture was firmly in favour. Easier mortgages meant that money could be raised in hard times without having to sell parts of the estate. The result was that there were fewer and wealthier landlords. The Duke of Newcastle in 1714 had estates in twelve different counties with an annual income of £40,000; the Duke of Bedford owned nearly the whole of the county of his title. Burke told the Duke of Richmond that he and his fellow aristocrats "are in my eye the great oaks that shade a country, and perpetuate your benefits from generation to generation."

It was hard to enter this exclusive coterie of "great oaks." The strength of the English aristocracy has always been partly a result of its ability to absorb new blood; but although this was theoretically possible during the first half of the eighteenth century, the vast wealth of the great landowners made their class virtually inaccessible to new recruits. The first two Georges created few peers, and most of those were Irish titles. The Glorious Revolution of 1688 had deprived the crown of its right to grant lands and titles to its favourites. Nor was it any longer so easy for those who made money in commerce to buy land. As law and custom prevented existing landowners from breaking up estates, there were fewer acres on the market. And estates were still a necessary condition of title. Sara Churchill advised her husband John against accepting the dukedom offered by Queen Anne to mark his victories against France, as he had too little land or money to bear the burden of a title. Only with a pension and an estate at Woodstock from the Queen and a grant from

The Churchill family— the dukes of Marlborough John Churchill, created first Duke of Marlborough (above) in 1702 for his military services to England. The family played an important part in eighteenth and nineteenth century politics, the most influential member being Lord Randolph Churchill, third son of the seventh duke. Lord Randolph's son Winston Churchill had a long political career during which, as Prime Minister, he led Britain through the Second World War.

Syon House, seat of the Duke of Northumberland

Parliament to build Blenheim Palace did Churchill feel able to become Marlborough. A few other naval and military leaders were honoured: General Howe won an earldom; Admiral Hood the son of a Somerset vicar, a viscountcy and Admiral Hawke a barony.

The law, too, with its profitable fees, could be a route into the peerage. Lord Chancellor Philip Yorke was created Earl of Hardwicke in 1754. The profits of government office could also elevate a shrewd man. James Brydges, fourth son of a poor Hertfordshire gentleman, is the prime example here. He found himself a job as clerk in a minor government department and worked himself up to become Paymaster to the Queen's forces abroad. The salary and allowances of the Paymaster were worth £4,000 a year. But the incumbent was entitled to the interest on the balance of money in his hands and to any profit he might make by its investment or from commissions on foreign loans. Having made his profit, Brydges married into a poor but noble family whose ancestral home, Cannons, he rebuilt. With money and estate he became the Earl of Carnarvon, then the Duke of Chandos.

These generals, admirals, lawyers and officials who were welcomed into the peerage were the exceptions. Others who achieved riches and managed to buy estates, like the East India merchants were not readily accepted: Robert Clive (of India) was given only an Irish peerage; William Pitt's grandfather spent £100,000 on ten thousand acres but remained a commoner. It was Pitt's political talents, not his inherited land, which turned him from "the great commoner" into the Earl of Chatham. It was easier to rise by marriage than merit. Through his wife Mary Davies, a London heiress, Sir Thomas Grosvenor added to his Cheshire estates all the land in London between Oxford Street and

Chelsea. His wealth brought him the earldom, and his heirs the dukedom, of Westminster.

Marriage among themselves was an accepted method of increasing the wealth and consolidating the estates of the great families. The Duke of Newcastle's £40,000 annual income came partly from the rents of the Clare property; his father, Sir Thomas Pelham, had married Lady Grace Holles, daughter of the third Earl of Clare. Most of the 150 wealthiest aristocratic families were linked by marriage to several others, enhancing the impression of an exclusive group. But the number of landed heiresses was limited. The richest available wife was now often a merchant's daughter. The Earl of Bedford married his grandson Wriothesley Russell to Elizabeth Howell, granddaughter of Sir Josiah Childe, chairman of the East India Company. The hopes of the richly endowed daughters of city men were satirized by the playwrights of the day. In Colman and Garrick's *The Clandestine Marriage* of 1766, a merchant's daughter dreams of the future: "Oh, how I long to be transported to the dear regions of Grosvenor Square, far, far from the dull districts of Aldersgate, Cheap, Candlewick and Farringdon... My heart goes pit-a-pat at the very idea of being introduced at court! Gilt chariot! Laced liveries! And then at dinner, instead of my father perpetually asking 'Any news upon Change?' to say to some other woman of quality 'Was your ladyship at the Duchess of Rubbers last night?'"

Links had already been forged between the City and the lesser aristocracy. A good county family like the Actons of Shropshire who could boast a baronetcy were related to the goldsmith Actons of Leadenhall Street and to the linen draper Gibbons. The eighteenth-century aristocracy did not feel itself to be above commerce. The French nobility were forbidden to take part in trade or industry and so became an elite dangerously isolated from the rest of society; but many of the English aristocracy accepted commerce as a useful and exciting way of bolstering their incomes. Indeed, their younger sons, deprived by primogeniture of the chance of inheriting estates, were forced to enter the professions or commerce. They may have been reluctant to accept the East India nabobs into their ranks; this did not stop them from taking advantage of growing trade. After the Duke of Bedford had married his grandson to Josiah Childe's heiress he lost no time in joining his new relatives in profitable commercial enterprises. On the Howell property at Rotherhithe he built wet and dry docks where two new ships, the *Tavistock* and the *Streatham*, were launched on the route to the East Indies.

The Russells were typical of the nobility in their willingness to invest in new commercial and industrial developments. They took advantage of the introduction of modern methods of credit. The new joint stock companies (companies issuing shares) were risky and could end in a financial scandal like that of the South Sea Bubble (1720); but they were the means of raising money for such developments as paper-making and they needed the sort of capital the nobility could provide. When the Earl of Sunderland died in 1722 he had £75,000 invested in stocks and

George I (1714–27)

William Pitt, Earl of Chatham

shares. The Duke of Chandos lost £700,000 in the South Sea Bubble; but he could still afford shares in the Covent Garden Playhouse as well as investments in a glass works, a soap factory and a distillery. He invested in coal mines on his estates just as the Marquess of Bute tapped the coal on his Welsh property. The difficulties of transport on the rutted muddy roads turned the more enterprising nobles into canal builders. The Duke of Bridgewater's famous canal carried coal from his Worsley mines to the growing town of Manchester. In 1773 the Earl of Thanet built the Skipton Castle Canal to carry lime and limestone from his estates to join the Leeds and Liverpool Canal.

Younger sons of the aristocracy entered such professions as the law. A lawyers office

The Duke of Bridgewater's canal

Industrial and Agricultural Revolutions

The landed aristocracy did not keep their position as leaders of industry for long. As the industrial revolution progressed the new commercial class gained enough capital to invest in new enterprises; they also acquired the technical knowledge which the landlords lacked. But the initial capital and enthusiasm had come from the land and the nobility. The same was true of the agricultural revolution. In Charles II's reign (1660–85) scientific knowledge had been applied to the improvement of livestock, the allocation and rotation of crops. It was the wealthy landlords who could now afford the capital to introduce the new methods. The second and third Earls of Egremont converted 800 acres of Petworth Park into a model farm, introducing new tools and new methods of drainage and stock breeding. At Wentworth the Marquess of Rockingham farmed 2,000 acres himself, experimenting with lime and manure to improve his turnip yield. Lord Townshend became even more famous for turnips when he used them in rotation with three other crops. Even his Prime Minister brother-in-law, Sir Robert Walpole, used to open letters from the steward of his Norfolk estates before the State papers, so keen was every landowner's interest in the new agriculture.

The new agricultural methods all involved the enclosure of open land – at first by mutual agreement, then by Acts of Parliament – to form compact tenant farms. The wealthy tenant farmers, after the initial impetus of the agricultural revolution, were as responsible for the agricultural improvements and discoveries as the dukes and earls who have largely received the credit. During the eighteenth century the face of the country was changed as the huge open fields and commons disappeared to be replaced by compact fields surrounded by neat hedges. The landlords have been blamed for causing poverty in the countryside by their enclosures but the rise in population – it doubled from five to ten millions during the century – was far more to blame. The aristocratic landowners certainly enclosed their land for profit: Thomas Coke of Holkham, the future Earl of Leicester, raised his rents from £2,200 to £20,000 a year in the forty years after enclosing his land. But they were not too harsh as landlords and were usually on good terms with their tenant farmers. The Duke of Ancaster thought it unfair to raise rents immediately after enclosure and waited three years before doing so.

Rents were rising in the towns as well as the country. As commerce and industry grew – the labour market was fed by poor country people forced into the towns – so did the demand for urban land. Dukes and earls whose estates bordered the old town centres suddenly found these a valuable source of income. As Cardiff changed from a little fishing village into a city with docks, mills and factories the Marquess of Bute became even wealthier. Those with land near Westminster and the City of London were even luckier. The Earl of Bedford suddenly realized what a splendid dowry Lady Rachel Wriothesley had brought the Russell family in the manors of Bloomsbury and St. Giles. In 1775 he built Bedford Square – then Russell and Woburn Squares – with their solidly proportioned town houses. Similar houses went up on the estates of Robert Harley, Earl of Oxford, lining Mortimer, Wimpole and Harley Streets. In 1826 Parliament passed a private act allowing Lord Grosvenor, Earl of Westminster, to develop his estates at Westminster and Belgravia. He drained the area and built Grosvenor, Eaton and Belgrave Squares.

Thomas Coke, first Earl of Leicester of Holkham

The South Sea Bubble

Unenclosed land was fenced around by aristocratic landowners

Eaton Square

Grosvenor Square

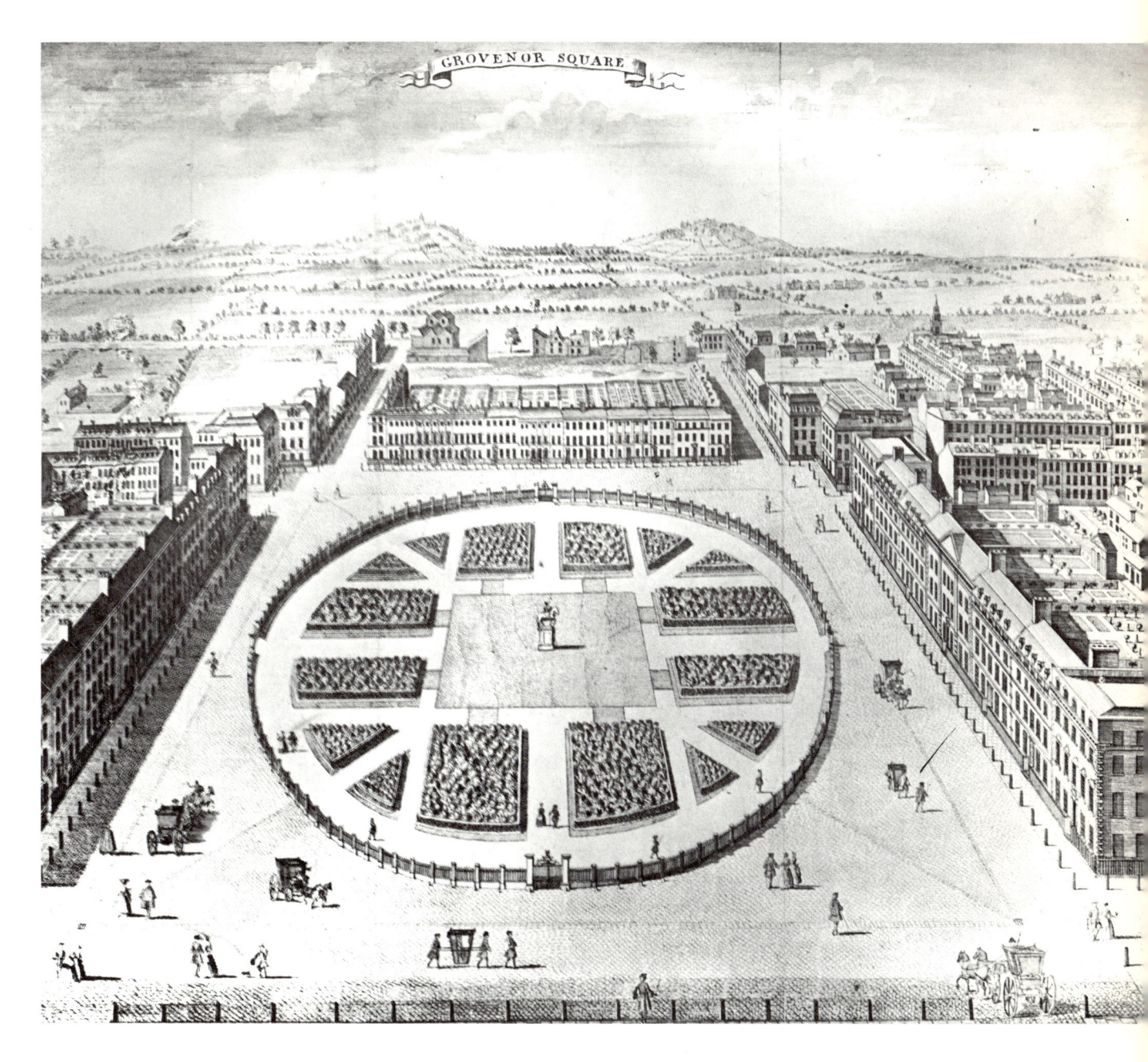

Political Leadership

The aristocrats were farmers, industrialists, speculators and property developers. But above all they formed the governing class. They had put first Dutch William and then George I on the throne. Now that the Hanoverians were firmly established and the support of the crown by the peers an accepted fact of life, political loyalties were decided less by party and principle than by family and personal loyalties. The rate of inter-marriage among the nobility was therefore important politically. When Lord John Russell formed his government in 1846 his opponents complained that it was composed mainly of his cousins. Government was

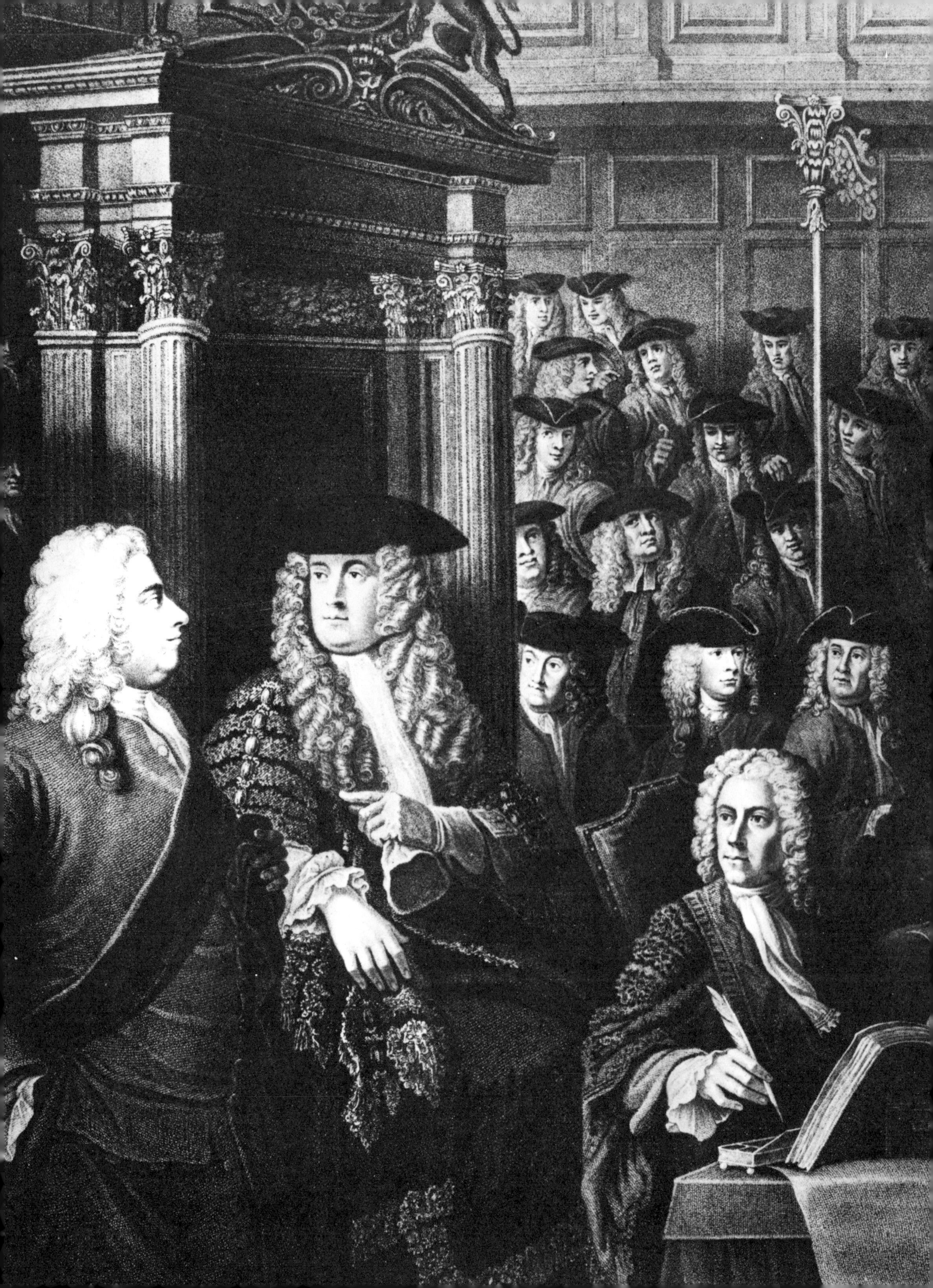

by faction or group; the art of government was to obtain and keep the royal favour and to control Parliament. The House of Commons was therefore filled with groups of relatives or loyal supporters of the great magnates who could afford to send them there. For the so-called "rotten" or "pocket" boroughs returned members at the behest of the local lord. Few but the wealthiest landowners could afford the expense of a contested election. The Duke of Bedford's agents declared unashamedly at an election on the Duke's estates in 1727 that they knew it "was to be bought and they would buy it, whatever the cost . . . 400 votes at four guineas each, and declared they would outbid their opponents as far as twenty guineas a man." In 1765 thirty-one aristocratic families returned a quarter of the House of Commons. The historian Sir Lewis Namier's detailed analysis of Members of Parliament shows how efficiently the system was used. He may have over emphasized the part played by party politics in eighteenth-century life; but he has scotched forever Macaulay's picture of the post-1688 aristocrat ruling according to a

Sir Robert Walpole, 1st Earl of Orford

Left The House of Commons. Voters returned members nominated by the local lord

Venice was one of the places visited by young noblemen on their European "grand tour"

Somerset House, London, one of the centres of aristocrats' social life in town

new Whig ideology of individual liberty and the sovereignty of Parliament.

As well as dominating the Lords and returning Members of Parliament the great noble families filled the offices of state. In 1726 a quarter of the 150 leading peers held administrative office either in the government or at court. Such office could be extremely lucrative. The Holland as well as the Chandos family fortune derived from the Paymaster Generalship. Daniel Finch, second Earl of Nottingham, acquired £50,000 in his six years as Secretary of State. These sums swelled the incomes drawn by the aristocracy from their estates and speculations: by the 1830s the first Earl of Durham considered that a man could "jog along at £40,000 a year."

Any office – whether in politics, the church, the army or the navy – not filled by the peers themselves was held by their relatives or dependents. The patronage of a great wealthy family was the first necessity for an aspiring politician. It had replaced the old crown patronage. Without the support of the Duke of Newcastle and the Pelham and Granville families, Sir Robert Walpole could not have won and kept his position as Prime Minister. William Pitt's career depended at first on his friendship with the Grenvilles, sealed by his later marriage to their sister. Once in power a minister had at his disposal the patronage which enabled him to keep his following and control the Commons. It brought him and his family riches and titles. Walpole could build great country houses, procure a barony for his eldest son and valuable sinecures for the others. The best sign of the political morality current in the

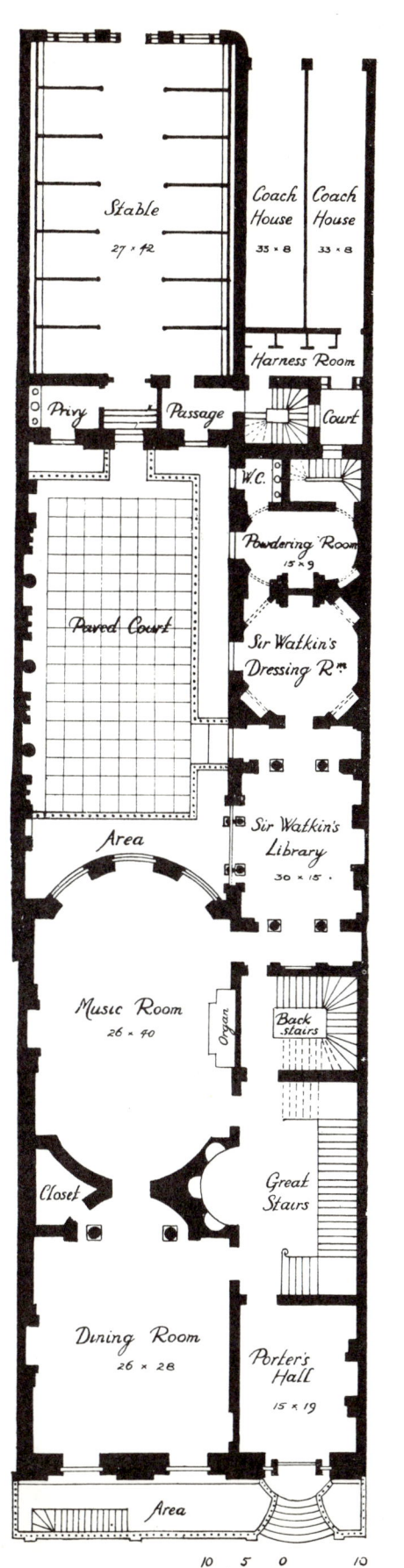

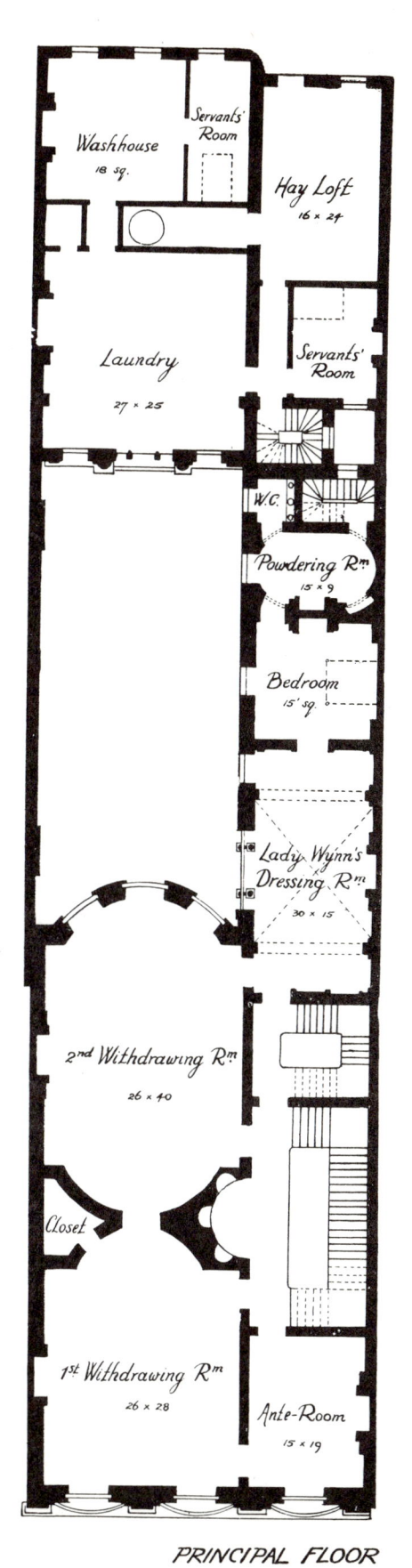

Plan of a typical large London house

PRINCIPAL FLOOR

83

eighteenth-century was the consternation which greeted Pitt's refusal to profit financially from any government office.

Members of the aristocracy were brought up to believe that they were England's natural rulers. Their education gave them the necessary confidence for this role and marked them out as an elite. Only a wealthy lord could afford to send his sons to Eton and Oxford and then on the grand tour. Lord Chandos' son spent £400 a year while at Oxford; a modest two- or three-year European tour cost between £3,000 and £4,000 while a few aristocrats, like the Duke of Kingston, spent £40,000 on an extended trip of ten years. Charles James Fox, Lord Holland's son, is said to have got through £16,000 in ten days at Naples. The content of the young noble's education was limited mainly to Latin studies. But on his grand tour he could absorb European culture and return home full of confidence to take his part in governing the country.

Politics became a way of life. The Whig lord was often a minister, one of his sons a Member of Parliament, another in the diplomatic service or holding some government office. While Parliament was sitting the aristocratic family moved to its London house and the social season began. The centres of Whig social life – Devonshire House, Holland House and Melbourne House – were also the political centres where the policies of the various factions were discussed and decided. When the young William Melbourne was invited to dine at Holland House he knew he would be included in the informal councils over the port and

Aristocrats were renowned for their ability to enjoy themselves!

Gambling scene by Hogarth

that his place in the party was assured. Hostesses like the Duchess of Devonshire, her sister Lady Bessborough and Lady Holland could do much to help a young man's political career.

At their hostesses' houses the sons of the nobility talked and drank into the small hours. Their capacity was prodigious and they were proud of it. George III once remarked to his Lord Chancellor, the Earl of Northington, that he had heard he loved a glass of wine. The Earl replied "Those who have informed your majesty have done me great injustice; they should have said a bottle." After an evening's drinking the guests might snatch a few hours sleep at home, or even go straight on to spend the morning at their clubs. At famous London clubs like Almacks, Whites and Boodles they played cards for high stakes. One morning in 1770 Lord Stavordale lost £11,000 at Almacks. Fox had lost £140,000, mostly at cards, before he was twenty-five. When Lord Holland refused to pay his debts he borrowed from his friends, the waiters at Almacks and the chair men in St. James's Street. The young aristocrats gambled not only on cards but took bets on any subject under discussion; whether a friend would be wearing a particular suit, who would be given what appointment, or how a debate would go in the Commons. For while they drank and gambled they talked politics. And in the afternoon they proceeded to their other club, the Houses of Parliament. Politics and social life were hardly distinguished.

Houses and Gardens

The parliamentary session was short. Returning to his country estates the Whig lord did not forget that he belonged to the ruling class. As a lord lieutenant he was involved in local politics; as the owner of a pocket borough he had to fight elections; if a minister he could be recalled to London to attend a cabinet meeting. But the pace of political life allowed him to enjoy his estates while his income allowed him to improve them. Vast sums were spent on the new mansions which now took the place of the Elizabethan prodigy houses. The Marquess of Rockingham spent £80,000 on building Wentworth Woodhouse and £2,000 a year on its upkeep. Vanbrugh designed Blenheim Palace for Marlborough and Castle Howard for the Earl of Carlisle. Walpole employed William Kent to make the walnut furniture and John Rysbrack to carve the marble chimney pieces for Houghton, his Norfolk mansion.

The garden was almost as important as the great house. By the middle of the century the formal layout was giving way to a more natural effect with waterfalls, wooded slopes, ha-has and contrived ruins. William Kent introduced these ideas into Chiswick Park which he laid out for Lord Burlington in 1736; they were taken up by Capability Brown. Gardens were stocked with exotic plants and animals. Lord Chandos had nineteen gardeners at Cannons; part of their job was to look after his flamingoes from Antigua and his parakeets from Barbados. The Duke of Argyll brought back the weeping willow and acacia, and the Duke of Atholl the larch and the fuschia from their foreign travels, just as others furnished their houses with French furniture, linen from Holland, tapestry from Brussels, damask from Genoa and carpets from Turkey.

Dutch linen, Flanders lace and Italian silks were also used for the elaborate shirts and ruffles now fashionable. Indian cottons were popular because they were easily kept clean. Indeed, cleanliness became something of a fetish with the aristocracy. Baths were taken more often; perfumes and scented waters were used by both sexes. Lord Chesterfield told his son: "Washing yourself, and rubbing your body and limbs frequently with a flesh-brush, will conduce as much to health as to cleanliness. A particular attention to the cleanliness of your mouth, teeth, hands and nails is but common decency, in order not to offend people's eyes and noses."

Paintings were the most popular trophies brought from Europe to adorn aristocratic homes. Lord Dainlow bought a collection of pictures from the Duke of Orleans for £20,000 for Cobham Hall. Many English painters felt bitterly that they had to copy the Italian masters in order to gain recognition. Later in the century the aristocracy supported their own artists, continuing the role begun by the Elizabethan nobles as patrons of the arts. The Earl of Egremont helped Turner and Constable at the beginning of their careers, giving the former a studio at Petworth, as well as buying work by Claude and Correggio. Many nobles commissioned Gainsborough, Reynolds or Romney to paint portraits of themselves and their families. Musicians and writers were not forgotten. Chandos retained the composer George Handel as organist in his private chapel at Cannons. The Duke of Rutland supported George Crabbe, entertaining him at Belvoir Castle. In their London salons noble "bluestockings" like Lady Mary Wortley Montagu and Lady Suffolk entertained writers and philosophers.

Impressive though they were with their pillars, porticos, sweeping Adam staircases and art galleries, the great eighteenth-century houses were not too grand to be comfortable. The new sash windows with their large panes of glass made homes much lighter than the Elizabethan lattice windows; the use of light mahogany for furniture and larger panels for the wainscotting made libraries and salons far less oppressive. The many smaller sitting rooms were geared to a relaxed and private life. Their wealth and upbringing gave the aristocracy the confidence to enjoy their surroundings without pomp and ceremony. Indeed, a French visitor, François de la Rochefoucauld, was somewhat shocked by their lack of inhibition: "Very often I have heard things mentioned in good society which would be in the grossest taste in France. The sideboard, too, is furnished with a number of chamber pots, and it is a common practice to relieve oneself while the rest are drinking." Perhaps the length of the main meal was responsible. Taken at three in the afternoon, consisting of a choice of roast meats and poultry, pies and fish, followed by fruit pies, tarts and jellies and a dessert of fruit – including imported lemons, oranges, melons, dates and figs – it continued for two hours. The men might sit for as long again over their wine. They would then join the ladies in the drawing room for the tea drinking made popular by the Duchess of Bedford, and for a game of cards. A supper of cold meats was eaten between ten o'clock and midnight.

Chiswick Park, showing the cascade

Dining room, Luton Hoo, home of the Earl of Bute

The Gallery, Chiswick House, home of Lord Burlington

The Character of the Eighteenth-Century Aristocracy

The nobility enjoyed their food, their gardens, their paintings, their gambling, fox hunting, prize fighting and horse racing, their visits to the spas, their politics and each others' wives and mistresses with the same gusto and lack of moral scruple. Many of their favourite activities brought them into contact with the rest of society. All classes enjoyed the race meetings and boxing contests financed by the aristocracy: the Dukes of

The Derby, sponsored by the Earl of Derby

Cricket was played by the aristocracy in the eighteenth century

Devonshire, Grafton and Northumberland kept large stables at Newmarket. When the Earl of Tankerville added cricket to the sporting activities of the nobility in 1774 he took his villagers to play against other lords and their dependents. Thomas Coke of Holkham was on close terms with his Norfolk farmers, and the Duke of Bridgewater with the local millwright and engineers. Their involvement in the City and their patronage of the arts kept them in touch with the commercial and intellectual middle classes. They were part of society, not above the law like the French nobility; one of the latter was shocked that Lord Ferrers, after killing a servant in a brawl, was hanged like any common murderer. There was as yet no great resentment against them. After the painter Benjamin Haydon had visited the Earl of Egremont he said of the aristocracy: "There is nothing like them when they add intelligence to breeding."

Nevertheless, the nobility still thought of themselves as a distinct and superior elite. They wanted little real social truck with the professional middle classes. The Countess of Carlisle always addressed her doctor through an intermediary; Jane Austen's Lady Catherine de Burgh was typically supercilious towards the clergy. When the future Duke of Wellington called his soldiers "the scum of the earth" he was voicing many an aristocrat's view of the lower classes. Snobbish attitudes flourished within the aristocracy itself. Jane Austen's novels illustrate the growing gap between the immensely wealthy landowning dukes and earls and the lesser nobility.

The exclusiveness of the upper aristocracy was diluted by William Pitt's creations. Between 1784 and 1789 he made 109 new peers; the House of Lords was fifty per cent larger than the earlier eighteenth-century House. The main difference, apart from size, was that it became a Tory rather than a Whig stronghold. Years later Benjamin Disraeli might complain that Pitt "created a plebeian aristocracy and blended it with the patrician oligarchy . . . He caught them in the alleys of Lombard Street and clutched them from the counting houses of Cornhill." But in fact the new peers came from the traditional sources, swelled by the service honours following Pitt's wars. The only new British peer from commerce, Robert Smith (Lord Carrington), had given up his banking career and bought vast estates in Buckinghamshire and Lincolnshire before his elevation.

The character of the aristocracy was unchanged by the new creations, but a little of the old confidence was lost. The Duke of Wellington could still tell Harriet Wilson to "publish and be damned" when she threatened to expose him along with her other aristocratic lovers; but his disregard for public opinion was typical of the eighteenth- rather than the nineteenth-century nobility. The French Revolution had frightened them. They retaliated as a class by becoming more repressive. The mass meeting led by Radicals like "Orator" Hunt, in 1819 at Peterloo and the Cato Street conspiracy of 1820 dedicated to turning England into a Republic, showed political reformers becoming disaffected with aristocratic rule. The reaction of the nobility was Eldon's Six Acts, curtailing

Duke of Richmond and Gordon's hunting party

Execution of Lord Ferrers

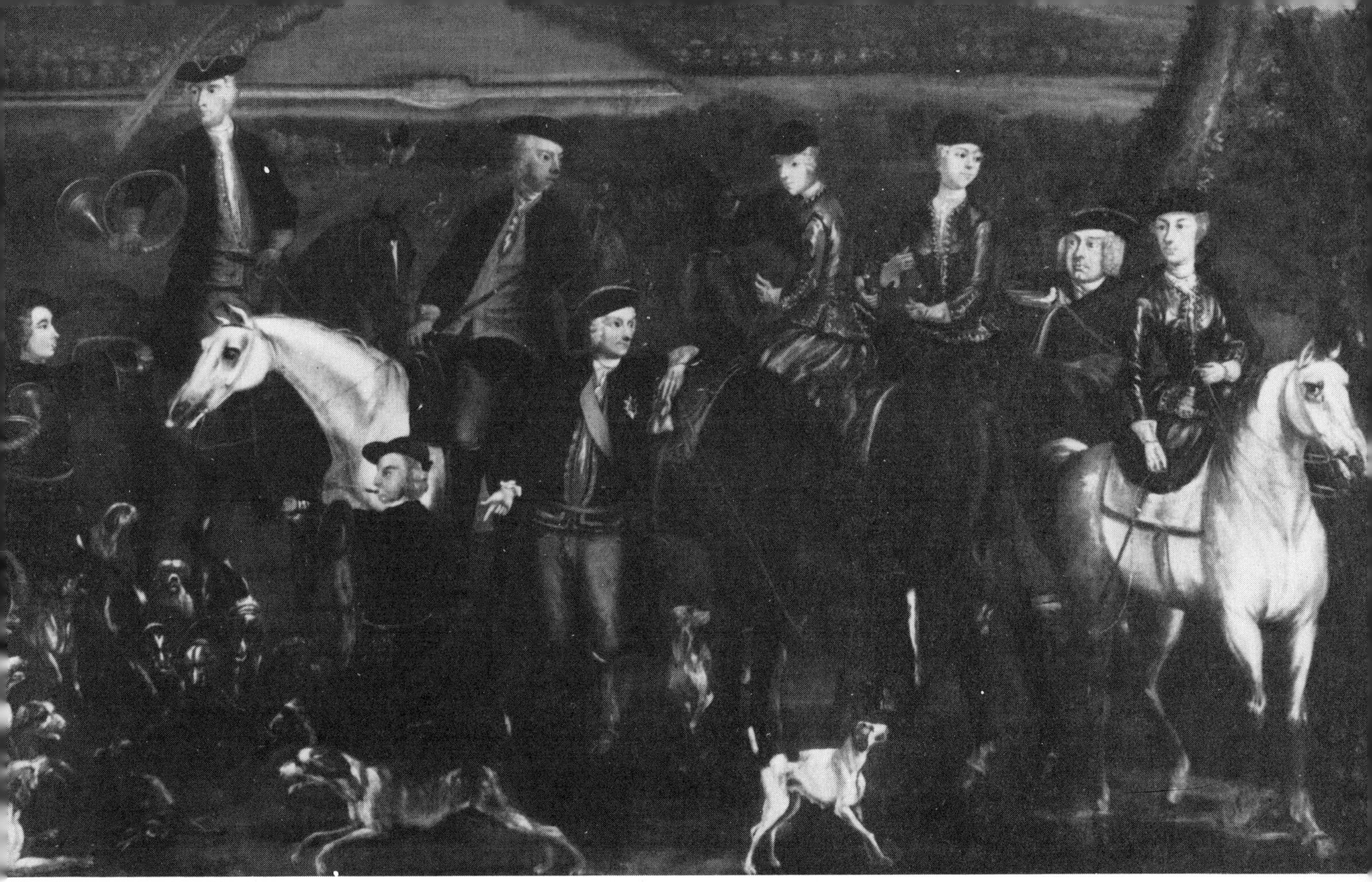

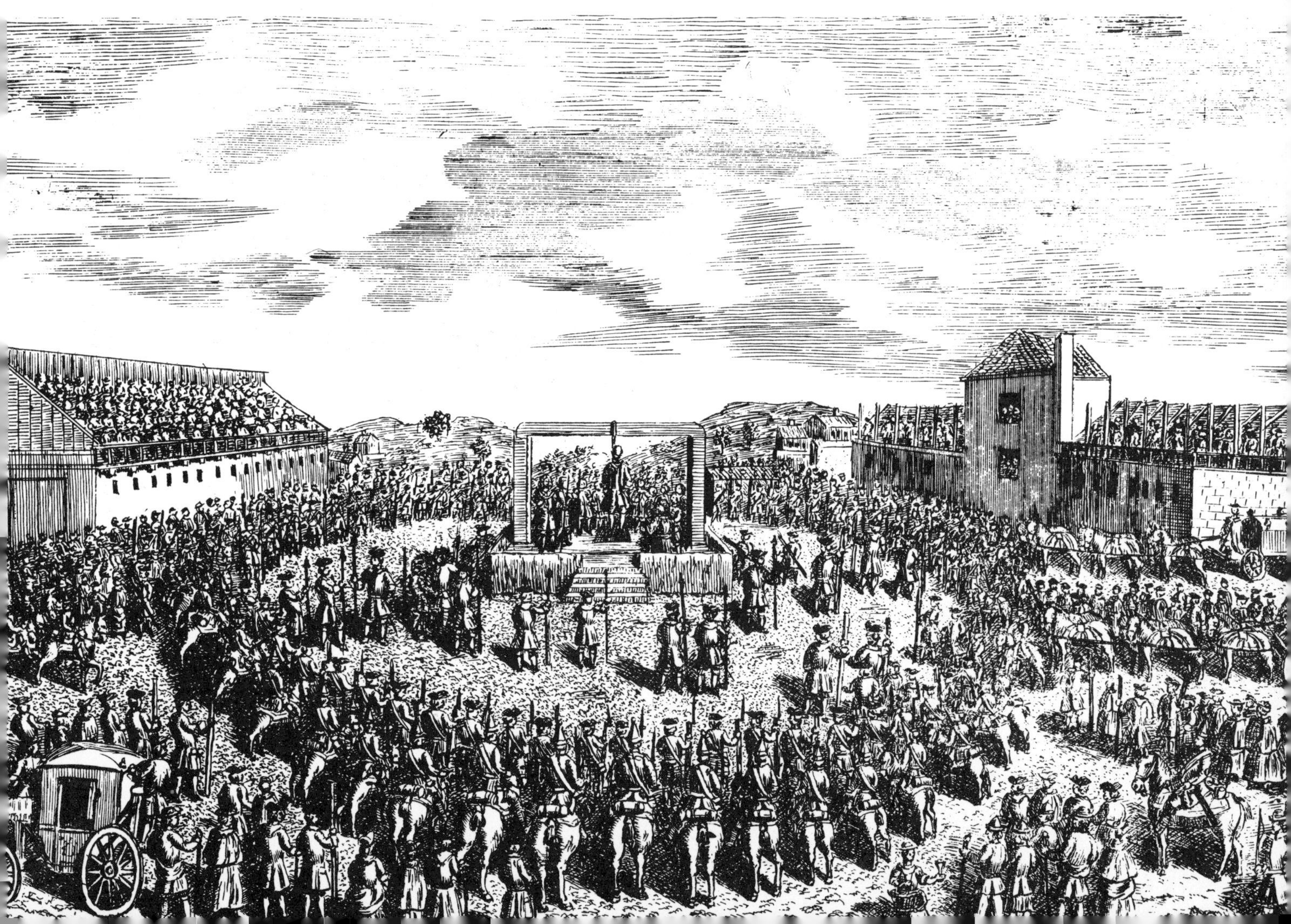

liberty of expression. But it was no longer easy for them to use their power to maintain the *status quo*. They had ruled in their own interest for over a century. When so large a proportion of the population earned their living from the land, the rule of the landowners – especially through protective measures like the corn laws which kept up the price of corn – could be seen as not only in their own but in the national interest. Aristocratic rule had been accepted without rancour. But the nation and the national interests were changing: the position of the aristocracy as unquestioned rulers was threatened.

Troops break up mass meeting at St. Peter's Field's, Manchester, 1819 (Peterloo). The aristocracy saw its privileges threatened by such meetings

6 Survival of the Fittest

An American, Ralph Waldo Emerson, travelling in England in 1847 was impressed by the estates of the nobility: "The Duke of Sutherland owns the county of Sutherland, stretching across Scotland from sea to sea. The Duke of Devonshire, besides his other estates, owns 96,000 acres in the county of Derby. The Duke of Richmond has 40,000 acres at Goodwood and 300,000 at Gordon Castle. The Duke of Norfolk's park in Sussex is fifteen miles in circumference." The number of people who owned small plots of land in England grew during the nineteenth century. But when Lord Derby set out to prove in 1872 that the land was owned by the common people he found that these new smallholdings only accounted for one-fifth of the country. His New Domesday Survey showed, to his own consternation, that England was still owned by an aristocratic coterie.

The noble's estate brought him more than farms, parkland, gardens and a country mansion. In 1815 it was still the territorial basis of local influence, giving him his social position in the country and political influence through the nomination of Members of Parliament. Its produce brought him prosperity. By the end of the century his political influence had been affected by the Reform Acts, his prosperity by the repeal of the corn laws (1846) and his local influence by the introduction of the county councils.

The Reform Bill receives the royal assent, 1832

The Reform Act of 1832

The 1832 Reform Act put an end to the rotten boroughs which had helped the eighteenth-century magnates control Parliament. The Duke of Wellington complained that the Bill would make the House unfit for gentlemen to live in; Lord Bathurst mourned that "the glory is departed." In fact the glory was quite a long time departing. For some time the type of men who sat in the Commons remained much the same as before 1832. But the Act marked the beginning of the end of interest and faction in the House. Members began to owe their first loyalty to their political party.

It was no longer so easy for the great magnates to return their nominees by buying votes. In the East Riding, Earl Fitzwilliam had to recognize

The Duke of Wellington

The Reform Act ended the rotten boroughs which had helped the aristocracy to control votes

Cartoon celebrating the repeal of the Corn Laws: "The Seven League Boots or Death of Giant Monopoly"

the interests of traders and coal merchants who were more concerned with railways and navigation tolls than large gifts or bribes. The Duke of Cleveland had to consider the voting power of Stockton and Darlington where middle-class property owners now had the vote. Many of the nobility were unwilling to take the necessary trouble to return the Conservative candidate when they felt that the Party had betrayed their interests. The Duke of Northumberland refused to use his influence in the 1868 election on his estates because Derby and Disraeli "have let the mob in upon us" by passing the second Reform Bill (1867). Such supporters of the old hierarchy as the writer and poet Matthew Arnold deplored the decline of aristocratic leadership. In 1861 Arnold wrote: "I cannot doubt that in the intrinsic commanding force of the English upper class there is a diminution."

It was expense as well as disillusionment which dissuaded the aristocracy from taking an active part in elections. Few were now willing to pay out sums like the £14,000 spent on the 1841 South Durham campaign. The main cause of their declining prosperity was the repeal of the corn laws in 1846. The middle class had won a share of political influence in 1832. They used their new power to force Parliament to end the legislation which had kept up the price of wheat and so profited the great landowners. The issue was so vital and feelings ran so high that the Conservative party was split. Benjamin Disraeli refused to vote for repeal. He forecast the decline of the landed aristocracy, as the urban interest flourished with the progress of the industrial revolution.

Like Wellington's prophecies after the first Reform Act (1832), Disraeli's for some time seemed merely eccentric. The effect of the corn law repeal was not felt for twenty years. Meantime the landowning aristocracy enjoyed much prosperity. Rents rose in the 1850s when three and a half million acres were ploughed for wheat. Agricultural techniques and estate management were improving. The Duke of Northumberland's agent, Hugh Taylor, turned the Alnwick estate office into a busy administrative centre, overseeing drainage and building superintendants. Smaller estates like those of the Earl of Pembroke and the

Aristocrats at an agricultural show

Marquess of Bath were also reorganized by agents. Nor were the resulting profits yet subject to estate duties.

The Railway Age

Farming was not the only source of profit for the Victorian aristocrat. This was the railway age. The new steam trains had to run on lines which cut through the aristocratic estates. The nobility objected to the trains disturbing their peace and views, but they realized that they could neither antagonize local feeling nor lose the income involved. The Earl of Pembroke refused to let the South Western Railway run three quarters of a mile from Wilton House but did not object to a distance of two miles. Profits were high. Between 1847 and 1851 the Duke of Northumberland received £23,000 from land purchase and compensation.

The industrial revolution demanded raw materials as well as transport. The nobility profited from the minerals they found on their estates. Previously, a few enterprising landowners had mined their own coal or lead. Now, outside capital and skills were available. Landowners preferred not to take the trouble or risks involved, but merely the royalties and rents. The Duke of Cleveland had an income of £14,000 by the mid-fifties derived from his lead mines at Teesdale and his coal mines at Durham and Wolverhampton. He also made a small fortune in 1867

Benjamin Disraeli, Earl of Beaconsfield

93

Many aristocrats profited from land purchase and compensation resulting from the new railways which crossed their land

The Grosvenor family—dukes of Westminster
Sir Richard Grosvenor of Eaton, Cheshire was created a baronet by Charles II in 1662. The family continued to take their seats in Parliament without great distinction. The eighth earl (above) was created a marquess in 1831. The title was elevated to a dukedom in 1874. The Grosvenor family have been astute in increasing the size of their estates.

selling some of his land outside Darlington for building. With towns spreading so fast, the development of estates happily placed near urban centres became even more profitable in the nineteenth than the previous century. The Duke of Portland developed Soho and Marylebone in London, including Great Portland Street and Portland Place. His London rents rose in 1844 to £50,000. Families like the Grosvenors and the Russells with valuable London properties became immensely wealthy.

The Homes of the Nobility

Extravagances such as carriages and liveried horsemen were cut down after the 1830s. This was partly from the fear of ostentation after the Chartist troubles (Radical riots in the 1830s and 1840s) and partly because travel was to some extent transferred to the new railways. But aristocratic homes were as sumptuous as ever. They were now built – or the classical Georgian and Regency houses were remodelled – on Gothic lines, in the current vogue for romanticism. As his rents from Eaton Square, London, increased, Lord Grosvenor added Gothic wings to Eaton Hall in Cheshire. A few favoured architects were patronized by the nobility. James Wyatt remodelled Belvoir Castle for the Duke of Rutland at a cost of £400,000; he built Ashridge Park with its turrets and pinnacles for the Earl of Bridgwater. Anthony Salvin reconstructed Petworth for Lord Leconfield, Longford Castle for the Earl of Radnor, and Alnwick Castle for the Duke of Northumberland. Jeffrey Wyatt did the same for the Marquess of Bath's Longleat and the Duke of Devonshire's Chatsworth.

Under the Gothic turrets new comforts were introduced. Alnwick had steam closets, hydraulic lifts and gas fittings as well as Italian carvings. Knole was warmed by steam and Tottenham Park by hot air ducts. When Hippolyte Taine, the Frenchman, visited several great houses in 1871 he was impressed with the vast meadows and parkland, the ancient oaks, the "embanked and cared for streams... made to form small lakes on which swim exotic ducks," and with the vast drawing rooms and conservatories. But most of all he appreciated the fact that, "Great attention has been given to comfort, notable in all that concerns sleeping, washing and dressing accommodation. In my room there is a carpet covering the whole floor, oil-cloth before the wash stand, matting along by the walls."

Such households were based on the cheap servant labour still available. Taine described how "a servant waits on you in the room four times a day. In the morning to draw the curtains and blinds and open the inside shutters, take away shoes and clothes and bring a large jug of hot water, and a linen mat for standing on; again at noon and at seven in the evening to bring water so that the guest can wash for luncheon and dinner; and at night to shut the windows, turn down the bed, prepare the wash stand, replace towels and other linen. It is all done with gravity, silence and respect." Many guests at a time would be waited on in this way. For the nobility loved to entertain each other. Lord Verulam, the Earl of Grimston, not one of the wealthiest of the aristocracy, regularly entertained the Dukes of York and Gloucester, foreign princes like Leopold and Esterhazy, his brother-in-law, Lord Liverpool, and his political associates, like the Peels. Prescott, a visiting American historian, found that a simple evening's entertainment at Alnwick involved a dinner served by liveried footmen off silver plate and a concert by musicians from London.

Many aristocrats owned more than one country home. They moved from one to the other, not to live off their produce as their ancestors had done, but to provide variety in their sporting lives. The Duke of Cleveland spent the winter at Battle Abbey in mid-Sussex, the spring at Ercall House on his Shropshire estate and later visited Raby for the grouse shooting and hunting. The Marquess of Aylesbury was always on his Yorkshire estates in August. The Duke of Rutland used Cheveley during the racing season because it was convenient for Newmarket. During Ascot the Duke of York was always at Frogmore where he entertained nine or ten dukes at a time. Hunting, shooting and racing were the favourite pastimes of the nobility. An outlay of £2,000 a year on his stables and £500 on his kennels was not excessive for a great landowner.

The main migration of the aristocracy was to London for the season. Everyone who was anyone lived in London from February until August, with breaks at Easter and Whitsun. Northumberland House in the Strand, Grosvenor House in Park Lane, Hertford House in Mayfair, were typical of the sumptuous town establishments built or remodelled

Eaton Hall, Cheshire

A footman

Dining room of Berkeley Castle, 1873, in what was the Great Hall in medieval times

Hunting, still a favourite sport of the aristocracy

How the poorest lived in nineteenth century England

by the nobility. The Londonderrys bought their house in Park Lane for £43,000 and spent £200,000 on improving and furnishing it. While in town they attended soirées, balls and operas, their clubs and Parliament. They mixed with artists and aspiring politicians who made their way into aristocratic and governing circles. The painters Joshua Reynolds and George Stubbs, met the nobility in their drawing rooms and were then asked to their country houses to paint their families and their horses.

It was not too easy to enter the salons of the wealthiest dukes. Benjamin Disraeli, Jewish and somewhat eccentric, was not at first asked to dine at the most exclusive houses and received few invitations to country weekends. But hierarchical attitudes were most obvious in the search for suitable wives for noble sons. The choice was made within a very limited circle; long arguments took place over settlements. The banker Alexander Baring's daughter married the Marquess of Bath, and he had to provide a dowry of £50,000. American heiresses were also expected to pay dearly for the honour of marrying into the British aristocracy. Leonard Jerome was appalled at the custom of allowing the bride so little of her own fortune. He demanded an independent income for his daughter Jeanette when she married Lord Randolph Churchill, son of the Duke of Marlborough. Such a union, and those with Jewish heiresses like Earl Rosebery's marriage to Hannah Rothschild, were in the old aristocratic tradition of marrying new wealth.

Few great aristocratic houses were built in town or country after the end of the 1860s. The great magnates could no longer happily afford

Shooting and racing, still aristocratic sports

The Cavendish family—earls and dukes of Devonshire
The earldom was given to William Cavendish by James I in 1618. William, the third earl, entered Parliament in 1661. His strong Whig sympathies led to clashes with the King. After imprisonment for debt he built Chatsworth House. He was created Duke in 1694. The eighth duke (above) became leader of the Liberal Unionist party in 1886.

expensive elections. The Duke of Marlborough was really grateful for his new daughter-in-law's contribution to the upkeep of his estates. The repeal of the corn laws had caught up with the nobility. In the 1870s poor harvests at home coincided with the opening up of the American West by the new railways. Cheap corn flooded the English market, bringing down the price of home grown wheat from £2.80 a quarter in 1867 to £1.36 in 1894. Between 1875 and 1885 a million acres of wheatland was left unploughed. At the same time fast ocean transport and refrigerated storage enabled cattle farmers in Argentina, Australia and New Zealand to compete with English landowners.

97

Ball given by the Duchess of Sutherland, Stafford House, 1873

Power and Influence

Farming, the old mainstay of the aristocracy, no longer brought prosperity. They looked elsewhere for income, to the stock exchange and industry. The Marquess of Salisbury invested in railway stock, the Duke of Portland bought shares in breweries, collieries, South African gold mines, and Burmese and Indian railways. For the Empire might provide the income that used to come from the country estates; a fair return, it was thought, for the service given by the younger sons of the nobility in administering it. Dukes and earls entertained the empire-builder Cecil Rhodes at their house parties and invested in Kenyan timber, South African diamonds and Rhodesian copper. They also took their places on the boards of the new companies set up by the London merchants and financiers. In the 1890s a company promoter, Hooley, made large gifts to titled aristocrats for the prestige of having them on his boards. By 1896, 167 peers held directorships. Some, like the Rothschilds, headed their own businesses which had brought them wealth, lands and titles. Others, like the Duke of Devonshire and the Earl of Durham, were ignorant of the businesses to which they gave their names. They were associating with the plutocracy which was replacing them as the wealthiest section of society. Land ownership was becoming less profitable than business deals. When the Liberal leader, David Lloyd

George, brought in duties on undeveloped land and increased death duties, the social advantage of vast estates no longer outweighed the financial advantage of breaking them up. By the time the First World War broke out in 1914, 800,000 acres had been put on the market and bought up by the middle classes.

But the great estates had been valued by the aristocracy even more as centres of local influence than for commercial profit. The role of the lord of the manor died hard; but it lapsed slowly during the nineteenth century. In 1834 Charles Grenville was staying at Petworth and attended Lord Egremont's open air feast for the poor of the neighbourhood: "A fine sight it was, 54 tables each 50 feet long were placed in a vast semi-circle on the lawn before the house . . . two great tents were erected in the middle to receive the provisions which were conveyed in carts like ammunition. Plum pudding and boiled and roast beef were spread out. Tickets were given to the inhabitants of a certain district and the number was almost 4,000; but, as many more came, the old Peer could not endure that there should be anybody hungering outside his gates, and he went out himself and ordered the barriers to be taken down and admittance given to all." In 1857 the Marchioness of Londonderry gave a dinner for the 3,000 pitmen of her estates in the grounds of Seaham Hall. But such jamborees were becoming infrequent by the mid-century.

There was some feeling among the younger aristocracy that the trend should be halted and the old paternalism revived. George Smyth and John Manners, sons of Lord Strangford and the Duke of Rutland, were at Cambridge together in the 1830s; they believed that an alliance between the upper and lower classes could best counteract the fear of revolution. "Let wealth and commerce, laws and learning die," wrote Manners, "But give us back our old nobility." His romantic ideas were the basis of the Young England movement. Disraeli, more hierarchical in his views than any blue-blooded aristocrat, supported it. But it was little more than an intellectual exercize and did nothing to stop the deterioration of the landlord-tenant relationship. One barrier between them was the new administrative agent on the estates who was more interested in efficiency than the tenants' well-being. Another was the introduction of Board Schools. These were set up by local education authorities between 1872 and 1902 and superseded those put up by the nobility on their estates. Deprived of such outlets for their feeling that power involved responsibility – *noblesse oblige* – some peers became leaders of social reform. The reactionary attitudes expressed in the House of Lords at the beginning of the century gave way to a more enlightened approach. The Earl of Shaftesbury passed through parliament the Factory Acts (1833, 1843, 1847) which improved working hours and conditions and forbade women and children to work down the mines. Another of his Acts improved mental hospitals.

Lionel Rothschild, Baron

Earl of Shaftesbury

The Transition to the Edwardian Age

Shaftesbury's active social conscience was typical of the Victorian

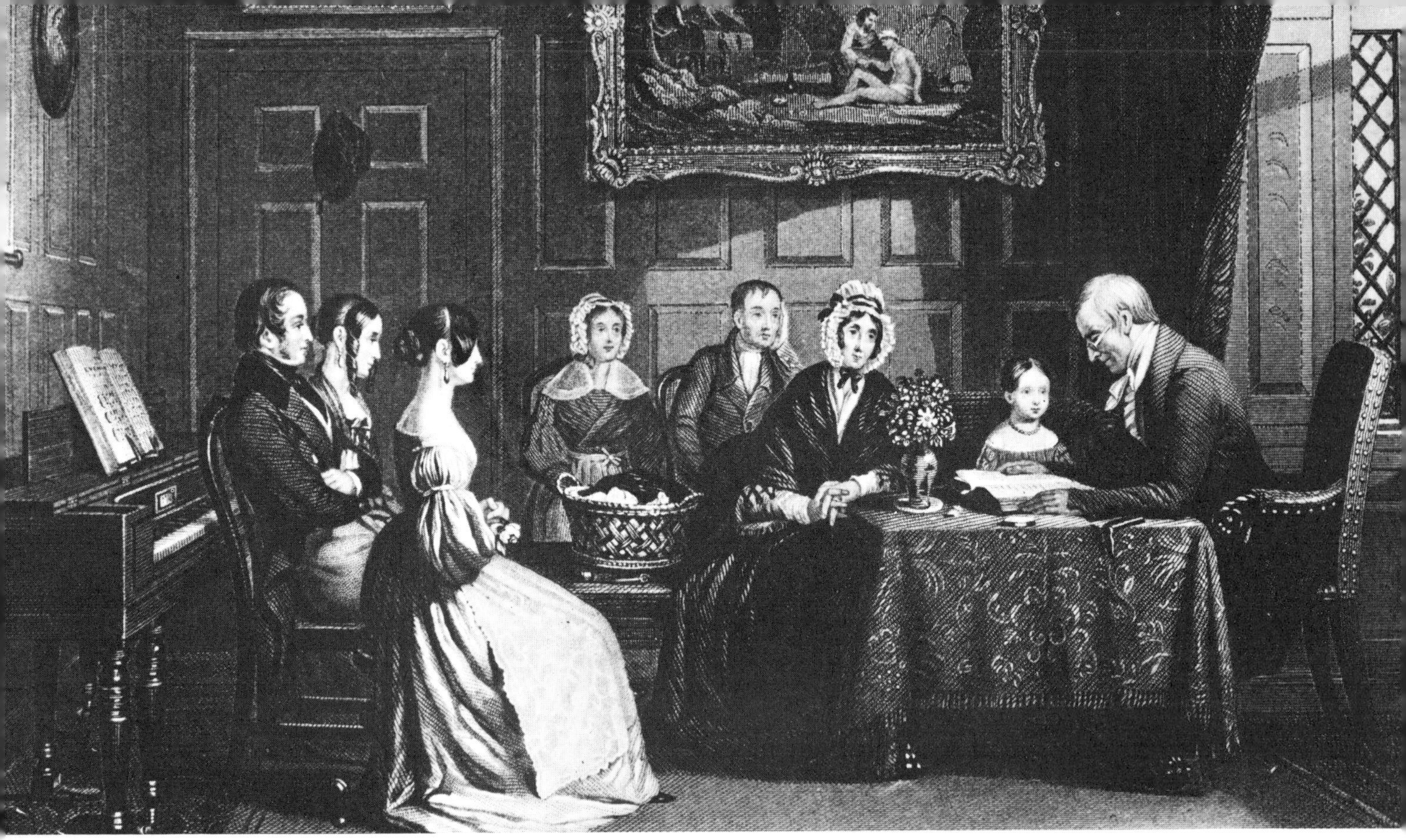

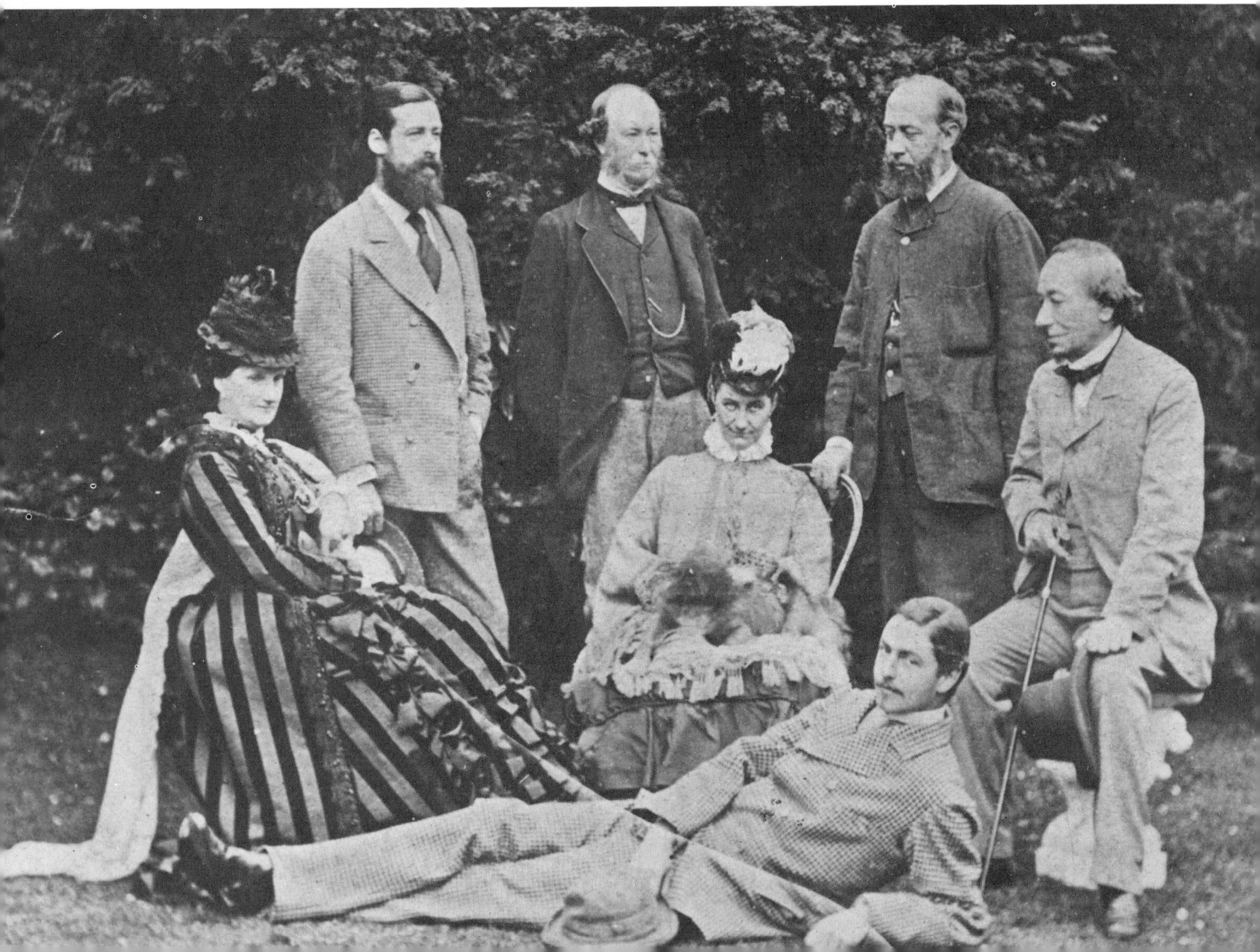

Sandhurst. Most officers trained here came from outside the aristocracy

middle and upper classes. It was very different from the uninhibited enjoyment of life characteristic of the eighteenth-century aristocrat. The plight of the new poor in the towns was partly responsible for the change in attitude; it was also an aspect of the spiritual revival reflected in the Gothic architecture of the time and in the newly popular evangelicalism in religion. Regency foppery and flippancy had given way to the stern morality of Queen Victoria and Prince Albert. By mid-century communal prayers were *de rigeur* in all upper-class households, following the example of the royal family itself. They were taken by the head of the house who exercized the authority over his dependents, extended family and servants that he used to have over his local country community. In a few cases this local authority survived the turn of the century. More often the Edwardian noble failed to retain his ancestor's position as an integral part of country life. He might spend the spring at Biarritz, the late summer at Marienbad, the first week of August at Cowes and May to July in London; he was not often at his country estate. When he was there he was less concerned with local affairs than with his guests. The Edwardian weekend house party was an important feature of aristocratic, indeed of political, life. The diarist Harold Nicolson described how, "Tea was served in the blue gallery. There were little ginger biscuits which one could only get from Biarritz and of which one kept a store in case the King came."

Careers

When King Edward visited the country houses of the aristocracy he could discuss diplomatic and military affairs, his two prime interests in government, as well as enjoying the company and shooting provided by his friends. For the crack regiments of the army and the Foreign Office remained the preserves of the well-connected landed families. Yet aristocratic leadership in the army and the civil service was gradually questioned and eroded. The Crimean War (1854–56) and then the Indian Mutiny (1857–58) taught the lesson that aristocratic blood

Opposite top Evening prayers
Opposite bottom Country weekend at Hughenden, home of Lord Beaconsfield (right, with cane)

Schools like Rugby (above) provided as good an education for the middle classes as Eton and Harrow did for the aristocracy

provided insufficient leadership to win a modern war. The army reforms of Edward Cardwell, Secretary for War, in 1870, obliged all officers to undergo formal military education at Woolwich or Sandhurst. The increasing complexity of government similarly demanded a more efficient method of recruitment to the civil service. In 1870 the Liberal, William Gladstone, threw open all branches of the service – except the Foreign Office – to competitive examination. The old aristocracy was horrified: academic success had nothing to do with leadership. But Gladstone took the advice of Sir Benjamin Jowett who had already started an experimental entrance examination at Balliol College, Oxford, where he was Fellow and Tutor. When Randolph Churchill failed to get into Balliol he entered Merton, a College more geared to the old aristocratic ways. Until 1860 titled undergraduates had worn mortar boards with gold tassels and were excused degree examinations.

The third traditional career of the younger sons of the nobility, the church, was the slowest to open its doors to the middle class. In the 1850s, two-thirds of the livings in the country were in the gift of the great landowners, going to their sons, who hoped eventually for bishoprics, or to their sons' tutors. But while he continued to appoint the local vicar the noble's influence as a feudal lord was ended with the setting up of county councils in 1880. The aristocracy no longer had the monopoly of the officer ranks or the civil service. The middle classes were well able to take advantage of their opportunity. Their schools – Charterhouse, Winchester, Rugby, Shrewsbury and St. Pauls – may have had less social cachet than Eton or Harrow, full of the sons of the nobility, but they provided just as good an education, perhaps better. Indeed, many aristocratic fathers realized the limitations of the teaching in these institutions and employed private tutors at home for their sons. Aristocratic daughters were less well provided for than either their brothers or middle-class daughters. Their education was often confined to a governess and the London season. Then they were presented at court, decked out in long white dress and ostrich feathers, and were expected to attend dances and dinners in noble drawing rooms until they found husbands. Meanwhile their brothers left Eton and Harrow for Oxford and Cambridge. Here they found middle-class boys whose fathers could afford the high university fees as easily as their own noble families. They had to compete with them for places in the civil service and commissions in the army. They were even forced to reconsider their attitude to Oxford as a place for social rather than intellectual pursuits.

New Recruits to the Nobility

A few of the middle class managed not only to rival but to join the aristocracy. The banker Alexander Baring became Lord Ashburton in 1835; in 1850 another banker, Samuel James Lloyd, was created Lord Overstone. It is significant that, before being ennobled, Baring bought 15,000 acres in Wiltshire and Lloyd a large estate from the Duke of Buckingham. Land was still generally recognized to be a necessary prerequisite for the support of a peerage. Admiral Lord Nelson and the Duke of Wellington were both given estates with their titles. The case for life peerages was argued by the government in 1856 on the grounds that while merit ought to be rewarded, a man "must be a fool to wish for" a hereditary peerage if he did not possess a landed fortune. Like William Pitt's creations, the 139 new peers who won their titles between 1833 and 1885 were nearly all from old landed families like the Cokes (Leicester), the Lascelles (Harewood) and the Lambtons (Durham). Although most had served either as ministers or Members of Parliament, only 26 of them failed to boast ownership of 3,000 acres. These were 14 lawyers, 3 generals, 2 governor generals of India, 1 diplomat, Alfred Tennyson the poet laureate, and 5 politicians including Benjamin Disraeli. And before he could become Lord Beaconsfield, Disraeli had to borrow money from the Duke of Portland to buy the Hughenden estate.

Like Disraeli and the earlier noble bankers, the Rothschilds in the 1870s and 1880s bought land at Aston Clinton and Waddesdon before

Overleaf Lord Salisbury speaking in the House of Lords

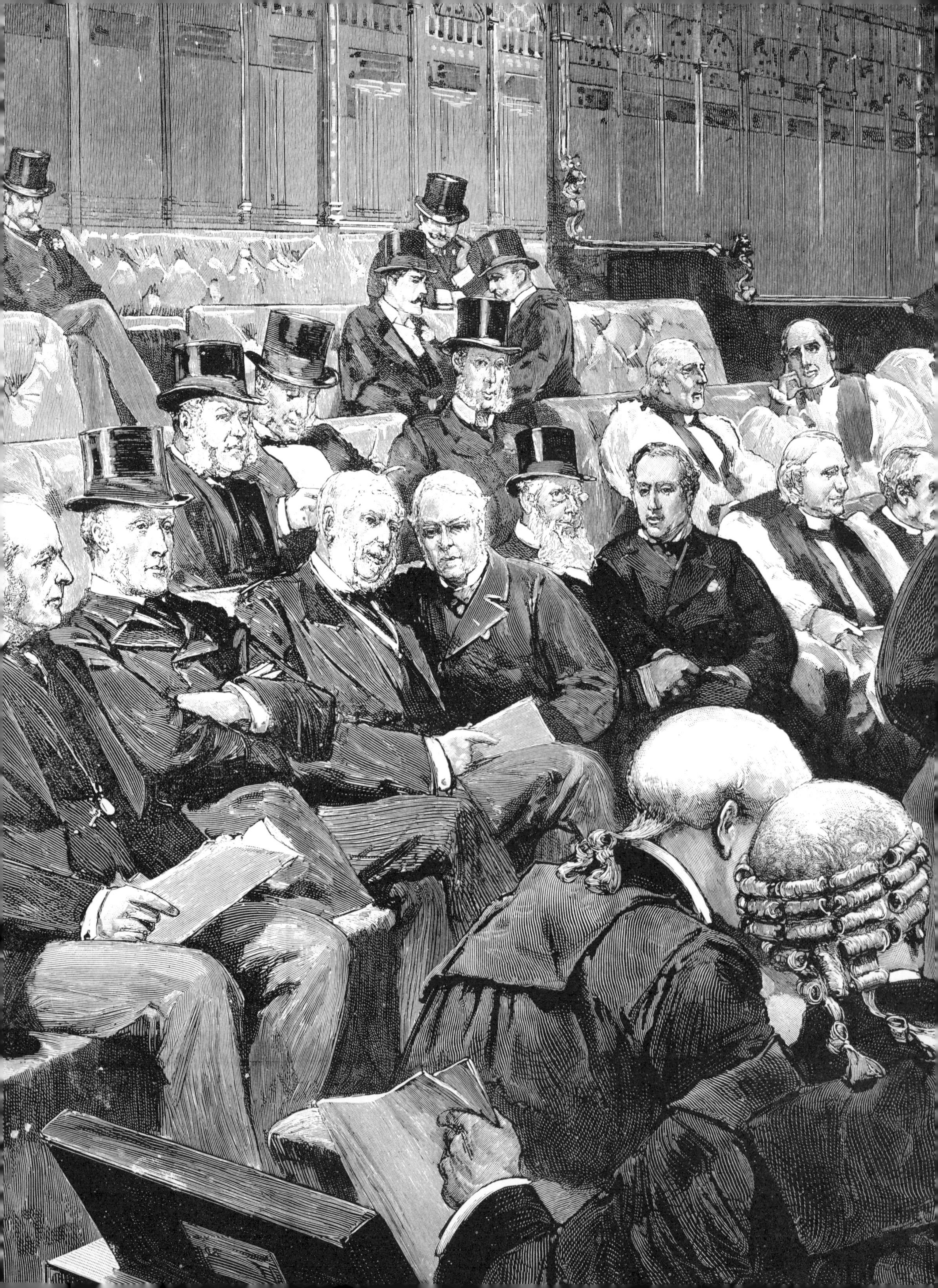

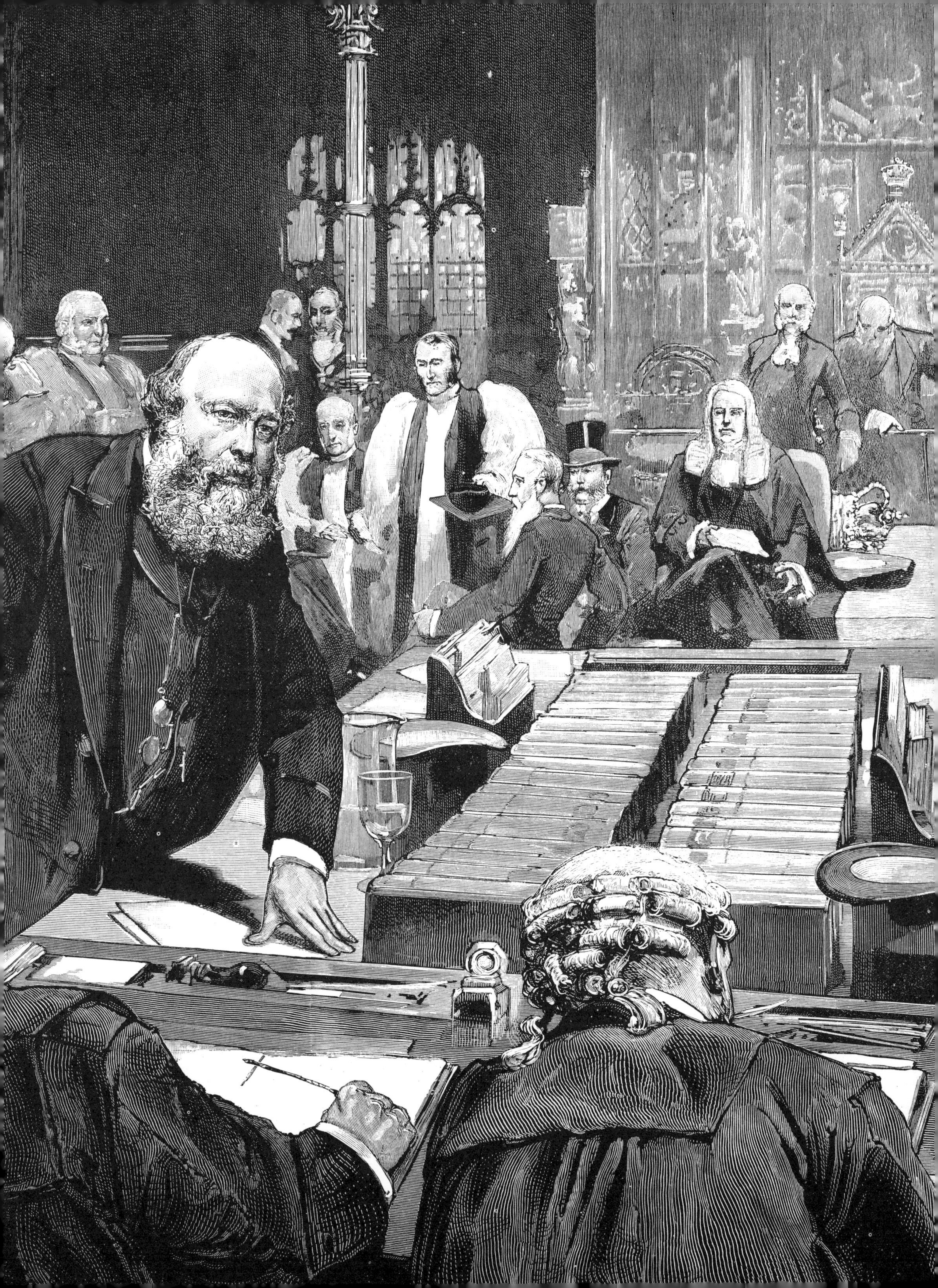

The Stanley family—earls and dukes of Derby
Thomas, Lord Stanley, was created Earl of Derby in 1485. Thomas, initially supporting Edward IV, changed sides several times in the Wars of the Roses. He later supported the accession of Richard III. Later, in 1485 at the Battle of Bosworth, Stanley took no part, despite Richard's summons, a fact which contributed to Henry's victory. Edward, the third Earl was a Roman Catholic and his sons tried to free Mary Queen of Scots from captivity. James, the seventh earl, a strong supporter of Charles I and II was captured and executed after the Battle of Worcester. Later earls took their seats in Parliament and played small parts in contemporary politics. In 1780 the twelfth earl instituted the horse race which still bears his name. The thirteenth earl was a keen amateur zoologist. Edward George, the fourteenth earl (above), led the Conservative (Tory) party from 1846–68 and was Prime Minister three times. The seventeenth earl directed recruiting in the First World War.

acquiring their title and marking the entrance of Jews into the aristocracy. As late as 1919, Field-Marshal Haig informed the Prime Minister that "unless an adequate grant was made to enable a suitable position to be maintained" he could not accept a peerage. A grateful nation gave him a stately home and £100,000 with his earldom. The later Victorian creations recognized the value of wealth other than the landed variety to the political parties. As industry and commerce became the source of riches rather than agriculture, so the wealthiest landowners were no longer the wealthiest citizens. Only then did the influence of the old aristocracy wane, making them willing to accept a large infusion of the new wealth into their ranks. Lord Salisbury, descendant of Elizabeth's minister William Cecil, made the brewer Henry Allsop into Lord Hindlip. A third of the creations of his second ministry came from trade and industry: Guinness the brewer became Lord Iveagh; the silk broker J. F. Eaton became Lord Cheylesmore; the wool merchant Samuel Cunliffe Lister, Lord Masham, and an engineering and armaments manufacturer Lord Armstrong of Craigside. William Gladstone's creations included the baronies of Ashton, Winterstoke and Rotherham, whose fortunes were based respectively on linoleum, tobacco and cotton. Shipping accounted for creations such as Inverclyde of Cunard and Pirrie of Harland and Wolff; newspapers for those of Rothermere and Northcliffe (the Harmsworth brothers). But while a third of the entrants to the nobility between 1886 and 1914 were from industry and another third from the professions, many were in fact younger sons of the nobility or landed gentry. Moreover, many of the newly ennobled industrialists, like Armstrong, bought large country estates. They were swift to adopt the country pursuits of hunting and shooting as part of their initiation into aristocratic life.

Lord Salisbury created the first industrial baron; Lord Derby passed the second and Earl Grey the first Reform Bills; many peers voted for the repeal of the corn laws in 1846. The ability of the aristocracy to recognize and accept the changing times enabled them to survive. Their concessions meant that the industrial revolution shifted the balance of power from country to town only slowly. Until 1906 peers were in the majority in every Cabinet. Even the Parliament Bill of 1911 – limiting the power of the House of Lords after it had refused to pass Lloyd George's budget – was drafted by a Cabinet containing one baron, one viscount, three earls and a marquess. The Home Secretary – Winston Churchill – was the grandson of the Duke of Marlborough. By the end of the century middle-class bankers and industrialists were as wealthy as the great landowners; middle-class intellectuals were taking over the civil service; the bourgeoisie were running the county councils. In London society Margot Tennant, the daughter of an iron manufacturer, was as celebrated a hostess as Millicent, Duchess of Sunderland, or Lady Dorothy Nevill, daughters of the Earls of Rosslyn and Orford respectively. Yet at the outbreak of war with Germany in 1914 only one-sixth of the hereditary members of the Lords were without large country estates; and peers predominated in the Cabinet. The aristocracy still held great power, wealth and social influence.

7 Partial Eclipse

Most of the Cabinet which declared war in 1914 were peers. Yet the aristocracy were no longer the real rulers. The commercial middle classes had already shown their strength; the rivalry between them was soon to be submerged as they joined forces to face the growing power of the trades unions. In this process the party alignments were re-drawn as David Lloyd George led a large section of the Liberal Party into coalition with the Conservatives to oppose the Labour Party.

Lloyd George and the Creation of Peers

Meanwhile the prestige of the peerage was undermined from within by new creations. When Lloyd George ousted Herbert Asquith from the premiership in 1916 he was very short of money. Many old Liberal supporters – with their contributions to party funds – followed Asquith into the wilderness. By selling new peerages Lloyd George raised nearly three million pounds. Of his ninety-one creations between 1917 and 1922 many were purchased by men of little merit and dubious financial background. Parliament passed an act in 1925 against such practices. But Maundy Gregory, one of the touts who had set himself up in a Whitehall office and sold baronies for £100,000 a time, carried on selling knighthoods and baronetcies until he was imprisoned in 1933.

Lloyd George's sale of honours was the most blatant example of a practice which had existed since Stuart times. There have been more subtle ways of buying one's way into the peerage. In the seventeenth and eighteenth centuries wealthy landowners could buy up seats in the House of Commons by purchasing rotten boroughs and then be rewarded with a seat in the House of Lords. Today, a generous record of donation to a well-known charity or party funds often results in a title. Peerages are awarded by royal letters patent from the monarch, but in reality they are in the gift of the Prime Minister who is a party politician. When George v asked for a mere knighthood for the inventor of the flying boat, the Prime Minister's secretary replied that there were inventors with prior claims for a title. The link between aristocracy and crown has weakened. Queen Elizabeth II's personal friends are drawn still from the landed aristocracy; but she no longer receives the same general support from the nobility that the pre-eighteenth century monarchs expected in return for title and land.

Victorian politicians had discovered how useful and cheap titles

David Lloyd George, Prime Minister, raised nearly three million pounds by selling peerages

Debating the Parliament Bill, 1911. When passed it limited the powers of the House of Lords to delay legislation

could be as rewards for past and continued support. Most new titles in the first half of this century – excluding those bought under Lloyd George – were given for political service. By 1956 half of the new peers had been Members of Parliament and over a third had been ministers; 39 per cent had worked in local government and 57 per cent in local party organizations. The peerage grew as politicians continued to use this form of reward and encouragement. Between 1916 and 1945, 280 new titles were granted. The Labour Prime Minister Clement Attlee created 98 peers in six years (1945–51), even beating Lloyd George's record of 91 in a similar period. Between 1950 and 1965 the 102 peerages that became extinct were balanced by as many new creations. In 1964 alone Labour produced 44 new peerages. By 1968 half the peerage dated from 1906 and only one-fifth could boast titles stretching back further than 1800.

The quantity of the new creations tended to devalue the titled aristocracy almost as much as the quality of Lloyd George's purchasers had done. Moreover, not only were there more relatively new peers, but also there were more lower as opposed to higher nobles. Most of the new peers were barons, with some viscounts. Earldoms by the fifties were reserved for wartime heroes like Alexander of Tunis and Admiral Mountbatten, and for retiring Prime Ministers; although Bonar Law, Ramsay MacDonald, Neville Chamberlain and Winston Churchill – and later Harold Macmillan – turned them down. The last Marquess, the Viceroy of India, Marquess of Willingdon, was created in 1936. Dukedoms are apparently reserved for royal princes such as Philip Duke of Edinburgh and Charles Duke of Cornwall, just as they were before Sir William de la Pole won his title. There have been no new non-royal dukes since Grosvenor became Duke of Westminster in 1874. The gap within the aristocracy between the higher and lower nobility, which began to open up in the seventeenth century, has widened as much as the distinction between older and newer creations. And since 1958 there has been the further distinction between hereditary and life peers. Of Harold Wilson's 44 creations in 1964, 32 were life barons and baronesses. Nobody has seen fit to create a life viscount, earl or marquess. The Labour Party has stated it will make no more hereditary peerages.

The Limitations of Political Power

But the loss of real political power by the aristocracy has not been due to the number or types of titles granted. The 1911 Parliament Act limited the power of the House of Lords to hold up legislation for two years. In 1949 this was reduced to one year's delay. In the case of a crisis, moreover, any government can use the threat of creating enough extra peerages to fill the Lords with their supporters. Few peers take much interest in their constitutional role. Attendance at the House has grown since they have been able to claim six and a half guineas a session. Only eight dukes spoke at all between 1955 and 1964. Their subjects included salmon, game laws, birds' eggs, pests, deer and trees. The highest recent turnout was for the vote against the abolition of hanging in 1958, though the decision was reversed seven years later. The real work of sifting information about proposed new laws, discussion and formulation of amendments is done by a handful of peers. Baroness Wootton wrote in a Sunday paper in June, 1962, that "these amendments, as everybody knows, have not the slightest chance of success unless they commend themselves to the government, and it is only a few of the minor ones that even manage that. The lordly mountain brings forth rather small mice . . ."

Another blow to the upper House was struck in 1963. The Peerage Act allowed Lord Stansgate to become Mr. Wedgwood Benn and other peers to disclaim their titles. Any politically able and ambitious title-holder now deserts the Lords for the Commons. This does not mean that some aristocratic families have lost all influence. The Cecils and Cavendishes are still powers in the Conservative party: Lord Salisbury's nod was necessary for many years before the Conservative party leader could "emerge." The Duke of Devonshire was an Under-Secretary of State; his aunt's marriage to Harold Macmillan benefited the latter's career. As late as 1963 the party chose the 14th Earl of Home as their leader. They soon changed him for a middle class grammar school boy, Edward Heath, but Home, ten years later, remains Foreign Secretary as Sir Alec Douglas-Home.

The Break-up of the Aristocratic Estates

Some of the most active members of the House of Lords are now the new landless peers. Those with estates to run cannot spare the time for parliamentary sessions. Government is no longer a pleasurable seasonal activity to be alternated with country life, as in the eighteenth century.

The Peerage Act of 1963 enabled peers to disclaim their titles. Lord Stansgate became Mr Anthony Wedgwood Benn

Then, only landed estates qualified a peer for his place in the Lords; now such a responsibility dissuades him from attending the upper House. In fact the necessary association of land with title is disappearing. Field-Marshal Haig was the last to receive a stately home with his earldom. The First World War (1914–18) caused the break-up of many of the old aristocratic estates. The Marquess of Bath sold estates in Shropshire and Hereford and 8,600 acres of Longleat between 1919 and 1921. The Marquess of Anglesey's 100,000 acre estate dwindled to its present 3,000 acre shrub nursery. The Duke of Rutland raised £1,500,000 by selling half his Belvoir estate.

Altogether, in the four years after the war, between six and eight million acres were sold – mainly to the sitting tenant farmers. This was not only because of death duties, payable twice over if the death of the title holder coincided with his son's fall in the war. Also responsible was the high rate of income and super-tax. The dukes were paying ten shillings [50p] in the pound, then considered exorbitant. If farm rents which had remained static during the war were now raised to an economic level, half the income would go in taxes. Selling was more profitable. Moreover, the costs of labour, estate management and maintenance had risen.

The smaller landowners, the untitled aristocracy or landed gentry, had to sell an even larger proportion of their estates. The condition for entry into *Burke's Landed Gentry* dropped from 2,000 acres before the First World War to 300 in 1935, and less in the 1952 edition. Some listed now as gentry have no land at all, just as Lord Norwich who does not even own the freehold of his garden in London is a landless peer. In general the nobility, with their greater resources, suffered far less than the gentry from heavy taxation and the depression of the thirties. The Duke of Newcastle even managed to build his estates up again in the 1940s. In 1968 Viscount Scarsdale took a reporter round his Derbyshire estates and told him: "When I succeeded to the title in 1925 the land was worth £25 an acre. Now it is worth £330 an acre as farmland and if you're selling for building it might raise between £1,000 and £10,000, there's such a demand for it. So you see, the whole estate is worth an incredible amount." Values have risen again since then.

The Church, Crown and Forestry Commissions, the army, the railways and Oxford colleges now own great tracts of the country. But the nobility are still the biggest private landlords. The richest estate in the country belongs to the Duke of Westminster. His agent runs a private plane to help him attend to the ducal properties in Cheshire, Shropshire and Scotland as well as the vastly profitable London property developments. The Duke of Beaufort owns 52,000 acres in Gloucestershire, the Duke of Devonshire 40,000 in Derbyshire and a Yorkshire grouse moor, the Duke of Northumberland 80,000 acres in his home county. As well as renting land to tenant farmers, each magnate runs his own farm. Good management and modern techniques ensure that these home farms are profitable. Many heirs complete their education at agricultural colleges.

The higher his title the more likely a peer is to be a landed magnate.

Lord Home (now Sir Alec Douglas Home) was Prime Minister from 1963–5

While many of the new life peers – industrialists, businessmen, academics – and some of the old aristocrats, are landless, the old assumption that a title needs land to support it has left its legacy. When a commoner is raised to the peerage he has to visit the Garter King of Arms who runs the College of Arms under the supervision of the Earl Marshal, the Duke of Norfolk. With his advice he chooses not only a name but a territorial attachment to his title. Roy Thomson the newspaper baron, for example, appropriately became Lord Thomson of Fleet, the now enclosed river that gave Fleet Street its name.

Country House Parties

A third of the aristocracy still have landed estates; one-half keep up one or more country residences. Edwardian style country house life managed to survive into the 1930s. In his memoirs Harold Macmillan described how "the country houses – Hatfield, Cliveden and many others – were the almost weekly scene of gatherings . . . Indeed, there was nothing so agreeable as the country house party in a large English house. There were no rules except the necessity of appearing at dinner and a certain bias in favour of turning up at lunch. Otherwise, in a large company the groups organized themselves for golf, tennis, walking, talking or quiet reading." The present Duke of Bedford's grandfather who did not die until 1940 continued to keep up the country life style of his ancestors. If you were a guest at Woburn, "you were allotted your own personal footman who stood behind your chair at meals, while a small army of another fifty or sixty indoor servants kept the archaic household going."

The Duke of Devonshire's family parties alone involved 150 people, because each son and daughter brought their maids and nurses with their families. The house parties at Cliveden, Hatfield and Chatsworth depended on the availability of cheap labour. Some of the upper class felt guilty about this extravagance during the depression of the 1930s. Harold Macmillan wrote: "Very often the transition from a few days at Stockton among my poor unemployed to the various degrees of comfort and wealth which we all either commanded or enjoyed left me with a growing sense of the great gulf." More typical was the determination of most of the aristocracy to keep their advantages, even to the extent of a flirtation with fascism. In 1938 Harold Nicolson met at his club "three young peers who state that they would prefer to see Hitler in London than a socialist administration." Such attitudes antagonized intellectuals and artists who were no longer, in the twenties and thirties, entertained by the aristocracy as their predecessors had been. Writers were encouraged not by aristocratic patrons but by people like Victor Gollancz of the Left Wing Book Club. Contemporary artists were unrecognized by the nobility, who preferred to stick to their collections of Rembrandts, Titians and Raphaels.

The war with Hitler (1939–45) interrupted the routine of the country week-end parties. Lord Kinross complained in 1939: "Now Britain is at war again. The war is costing her fourteen million pounds a day. In

Newspaper owner Lord Thomson (right)

Queen Charlotte's Ball

The present Marquess of Bath runs an animal park to help maintain his home, Longleat

taxation it is costing the Dukes and the Marquesses and the Earls as much as nine-tenths of each pound. The stately homes of England have become the stately slums, the stately nursing homes, the stately asylums, the stately schools. During the blitz more than a million children and hospital patients were evacuated from the industrial cities to their feudal drawing rooms and libraries and banqueting halls."

Aristocratic town houses were suffering the same fate. After the First World War nobles like Lord Derby and the Duke of Devonshire were still wealthier than the king. Buckingham Palace was just one of many great houses where entertainment was almost as lavish as it had been a century earlier. Lloyd George's taxes, together with increased wages for domestic staff, made their upkeep impossible. In 1937 the Duke of Portland mourned the old days when the great houses "were thrown open every season for large social gatherings... At present only Londonderry, Apsley, Bridgewater and Holland houses remain as private residences." The Duke of Westminster's Grosvenor House in Park Lane was knocked down in 1930 to make room for the Grosvenor Hotel; its grey colonnade is copied from the old mansion. Norfolk House has been rebuilt to house British Aluminium and there is a motor showroom in Devonshire House. Increased taxation after the Second World War brought about the end of any remaining great houses. The Londonderry Hotel was built on the site of the elegant Londonderry House. The only duke still to live in his family town house is the Duke of Wellington. He has a flat at the top of Apsley House; the lower floors house the Wellington Museum. Most of the aristocracy now have a "place" in London. But far from rivalling the Palace these are now flats in Grosvenor Square, Belgravia, Westminster and – more recently popular – Chelsea. Duchesses and countesses cannot give vast parties in them or dances for their daughters. Entertainment has to be provided in large hotels or smart restaurants instead of in their own ballrooms.

In the 1930s the presentation at court of 300 debutantes – eighteen-year-old aristocratic daughters – was the peak of the London season. Less well connected daughters had to find, and pay heavily, sponsors who had themselves been presented. After the Second World War high taxation and a Labour government threatened the season. The Queen's announcement that court presentations would not be continued after 1958 seemed a fatal blow. There are now more "coming out" dances than ever; but the girls who curtsey to a cake at Queen Charlotte's Ball are not all like those who used to curtsey to the Queen. They are the daughters of stockbrokers, industrialists and businessmen as well as of dukes and earls. The season has been taken over from the aristocracy by the plutocracy.

Stately Homes

It is partly the takeover of London by the new rich which encourages the older aristocracy to stay where possible on their country estates. After the War more of them had to be sold. In 1948 Finsbury Manor, the country residence of the Earl of Northampton was sold, marking the

The present Lord Montagu of Beaulieu (centre) runs a motor museum at his ancestral home

112

end of the prosperity which had begun with Lord Compton's marriage to Sir John "Rich" Spencer's daughter. There is a school at Stowe, an army college at Welbeck Abbey; Eaton Hall is demolished. But a surprising number of the old mansions survive and still house the descendants of the nobility who built them. The Dukes of Northumberland, Bedford, Devonshire, Norfolk, Marlborough and Rutland still live at Alnwick Castle, Woburn, Chatsworth, Arundel, Blenheim and Belvoir. In many cases only a small part of the house is occupied. Viscount Scarsdale lives in one wing of Kedleston Hall in Derbyshire and rents out three flats in another. Lord Pembroke occupies a few rooms at Wilton House. Moreover, 800 mansions are open to the public, making their owners eligible for grants from the National Trust to help them preserve their family heritage. At the end of the nineteenth century the Duke of Cleveland and the Earl of Leicester had shown select parties round Raby Park and Holkham Hall. Their motive had been pride, not profit. Heavy taxation then provided the incentive and the motor car and charabanc the opportunity to let the paying public in. Most peers hide as visitors wander through the corridors and public rooms, gazing at furniture and pictures and picnicking in the park. Others enjoy acting as showmen. When the Duke of Bedford succeeded to a four and a half million pound debt with his title in 1953 he set up a zoo and a fairground in Woburn Park. He shows guests round the Abbey himself and for £100 will even have dinner with them. To attract and entertain visitors the Marquess of Bath has introduced lions to Longleat and Lord Montagu has a vintage car museum at Beaulieu.

The stately homes have become profitable. They are one of many businesses in which the aristocracy is involved. Some, like Lord Redesdale with his Redeclean dry cleaning business, have entered commerce on their own. The Earl of Lichfield is a professional photographer. In 1966, according to a report in *The Times* 91 peers held one or more directorships of companies and 13 were chairmen of boards. Most were twentieth-century creations who may have earned their titles by serving in industry and then the political parties. But the older nobility is also active in business and in the City. Viscount Hampden, managing director of a merchant bank and director of an insurance firm, owes his title to his fourteenth-century ancestor; the twentieth Earl of Rothes is a director of electrical and insurance companies; and the title of the Earl of Verulam, now managing director of a metal company, dates from 1663.

Aristocracy and Plutocracy

With their incomes from their estates, their stately homes and their business interests, the aristocracy are still among the wealthiest members of the community. Half the private wealth of the country is owned by two per cent of the population; and this minority includes two thirds of the peerage. Among their possessions are sixty of the world's largest diamonds and some enormously valuable art collections. Their retinues

The Russell family—the earls and dukes of Bedford Dorset landowning family. John Russell created first earl in 1550. He arranged marriage between Mary Tudor and Philip II of Spain. He increased family lands, acquiring Covent Garden, London. The second earl, Francis (1527–85), a Protestant sympathiser, was imprisoned in Mary's reign. Became a Privy Councillor under Edward VI. Fourth earl drained parts of the Fens. William Russell, sixth earl, was created Duke in 1694. The family was important in the Whig party, throughout the eighteenth century. Francis, the fifth duke, introduced new agricultural methods on his estates. The family developed parts of London (acquired through marriage) resulting in Woburn, Russell and Bedford Squares. The present Duke (above) opens his home, Woburn Abbey, to the public.

may not rival those of their ancestors; but the Earl of Pembroke's complaint that he can afford to keep only a butler, a footman, a cook, two housemaids and several daily cleaners at Wilton indicates the surviving prosperity of the peerage. Weekend parties of twenty or thirty still take place regularly in about fifty aristocratic houses, especially during the shooting season. Some lords, it is true, are glad to claim their six and a half guineas attendance fee in the upper House; taxes may be heavy and death duties high, but these can to some extent be avoided by trusts and gifts made seven years before the death of the landowner. The Marquess of Bath has handed over Longleat to his son, Viscount Weymouth, in good time. If the Duke of Devonshire had survived two extra months his heir would have been saved two and a half million pounds in death duties. The Labour party's term of office was less of a disaster than the aristocracy had feared.

The peerage remains wealthy; but there are now more very rich men outside its ranks than inside. The newly rich rent grouse moors for the shooting season from the aristocratic magnates at £12,000 a year; they attend their house parties, bring out their daughters during the season and send their sons to Eton. But however much the plutocracy mix with the aristocracy, the distinction between them remains. It is difficult for the new men to get into the London clubs like Pratts, the Turf or Whites. The latter keeps its eighteenth-century reputation and is still the smartest gambling haunt for heirs of the peerage. A titled London hostess pointed out recently that "people with breeding know how to do things. Their houses are always just right and they know how to do the flowers and the food . . . You get some awful parties put on by people who have just got money but don't know, with tins of Beluga caviar all over the place."

Some plutocrats win knighthoods and even life peerages for themselves. It is questionable whether they can then be considered part of the true aristocracy. Nancy Mitford, the daughter of a baron, claimed that, "A lord does not have to be born to his position . . . he becomes an aristocrat as soon as he receives his title. The Queen turns him from a socialist leader or middle-class businessman into a nobleman and his outlook from now on will be the outlook of an aristocrat." He will certainly be a peer and sit in the House of Lords. But a new distinction is becoming apparent. On the one hand is the aristocracy, including the untitled gentry; on the other is the new peerage with their recent or life titles who sit more often in the House and venture less frequently into the country.

The plutocracy has merged more successfully with the aristocracy in London than in the counties. The new twentieth-century nobility often buy country houses; but for the first time they have not chosen to set themselves up as landed magnates. Where the old aristocrats still live on their family estates they still dominate the life of their counties to a surprising degree. They often choose the local vicar: 2,300 livings are still in the gift of peers and their heirs. Lord Scarsdale complained recently: "It can be very irksome finding the right man for the job. One usually consults the bishop about it – if one gets on with him, that is."

An Elite

Aristocratic influence is found in the counties in local government as well as in the church. Forty per cent of dukes, marquesses and earls and a fifth of the entire peerage are or have been justices of the peace, continuing the nineteenth-century tradition of service to the community or "*noblesse oblige*". They act as presidents of local charities and sports clubs, open fetes and give parties for their tenants. They lead the local hunt even though the riders now include the middle classes. The Marquess of Bath reminisced recently: "My father would have been quite shocked at the people who go huntin', shootin' and fishin' these days. Taking part in his exclusive sports indeed!" The Duke of Beaufort runs his private pack of hounds on his Gloucestershire estate. The Duke of Devonshire is Deputy Lieutenant, president of the Chesterfield Football Club and the Derbyshire County Cricket Club. He recently disrupted the local Tory party by refusing to continue their regular tea parties at Chatsworth because they insisted on inviting the right-wing Tory Enoch Powell to address them.

Aristocratic society still forms an elite in the counties. An *Observer* journalist commented that personal contact with the Duchess of Devonshire, "is still the social ambition of many of the wives of Chesterfield businessmen, although you would be hard put to it to find one who can claim to know her outside the line of duty." The elite nature of aristocratic society is obvious, too, in the make up of the smarter regiments of the army. In the Royal Horse Guards or "Blues" – the top cavalry regiment – between five and ten per cent of the officers are titled or heirs to titles. Membership of the elite means that a lord will get the best table in a restaurant and that his name is in demand for charitable and business notepaper and for company boards. The elite is held together partly through marriage. In spite of the penchant of lords in the Victorian era for American heiresses, and in the Edwardian years for actresses, intermarriage among the aristocracy is still very common. In the sixties fifteen dukes and eight marquesses were married to daughters of peers. Many of the older titled families are therefore connected. The Earl of Pembroke, the Duke of Buccleuch and Sir Alec Douglas-Home are all cousins. The Duke of Northumberland is related to a quarter of the other dukes.

Education, even more than marriage, preserves the aristocracy as an elite. More than half the sons of peers are sent to Eton. Here they are taught by a system different from that of any other school, play a special game of football and use a special terminology incomprehensible to any other schoolboy. They go on together to Oxford, most of them to Christ Church, and perhaps into a Guards regiment. Eton treats them like future rulers and they often adhere to the attitudes of their ancestors, who really believed they were the rightful rulers of the nation. In 1960 there were seventy old Etonians in the House of Commons. In 1965 they

The Duke of Devonshire opening an International Congress for the Welfare of Cripples

provided six of the nine contenders for the Tory party leadership. That same year Reginald Bevins, one of the few working-class Tories to reach a ministerial position in the party, complained of an aristocratic power group operating behind the scenes. More than a century after the first Reform Act (1832) he urged that "the notion that some people are born to rule must be destroyed." In 1973, judging by the background of ministers and shadow ministers, it seems that Eton and Christ Church no longer provide an automatic path to power.

The nobility are still a secure and self-confident elite. Unlike an aspiring middle class they are frightened neither of doing the wrong thing nor of public opinion. This may account for their high divorce rate. It certainly allows them to run their lives in unorthodox fashions. Lord Weymouth was educated by governesses, Eton, the Guards and Oxford according to aristocratic custom; for some years he lived as a recluse at Longleat, painting murals in oils mixed with sawdust. The Duchess of Bedford took up flying when she was sixty.

These eccentricities are in the tradition of the nineteenth-century Marquess of Worcester's stagecoach driving and the Duke of Wellington's confident "publish and be damned." However many dry-cleaning or lawyer peers there are, it seems that the aristocrat has not quite merged with the ordinary citizen. The press, which gives its readers what they want, is in no doubt about this. It is continually photographing peers riding bicycles and peeresses going shopping. Public curiosity helps to preserve the nobility as an elite. Nancy Mitford's book, *Noblesse Oblige*, describing the habits and vocabulary of the aristocracy, was a best seller. The rest of the nation was intrigued by her information, just as it has been by the recent downfall of the second Earl Jellicoe and the son of the fifth Earl of Durham in the so-called call-girl scandal.

The public loves its peerage and loves to try to join it. There is an enormous demand for titles every year. The list of recommended names has to be cut to two per cent before it is presented to the Queen. Industrialists, trade unionists and academics are equally eager to be ennobled. Artists and writers now accept the knighthoods their predecessors refused in the twenties and thirties. In spite of this apparent solidarity, however, the late nineteenth-century union of church, civil service, politics and intellectuals achieved through the cousinhoods of aristocratic society has vanished. The "old boy network" has given way to the "Establishment." Real power now is in the hands of career politicians, permanent secretaries of a civil service open to merit, trade union bosses, city tycoons and captains of industry. The old wealth of the nobility is challenged by the new plutocracy, its old power by the meritocracy. But it retains great riches, social cachet and some influence in the Tory party at least. The custom of primogeniture, its own flexibility in accepting both new men and compromises, and the support of public opinion has enabled it to survive from the eleventh to the twentieth century. It will continue to do so until the hereditary peerage dies out. Even then the English will still love their lords.

Glossary

ANGEVINS   Members of the house of Plantaganet from Anjou in north-west France. The English kings from Henry II to Richard II were members of this house.

ANJOU   Area in north-west France belonging from the tenth century to the house of Plantagenet. It was controlled by the English kings from 1156 to 1205.

ATTAINDER   The punishment for treason or rebellion against the king. The rebel lost his rights, possessions and usually his life.

BARON   A rank in the peerage.

BARONET   The lowest titled order in the peerage.

CASTELLAN   Governor of a castle.

CHARTISTS   Supporters of nineteenth-century working-class movement for political reforms and greater equality of suffrage.

COLLEGE of ARMS   The only body in the country entitled to draw up titles and coats of arms for members of the peerage.

COMPTROLLER   Traditional spelling for "controller", still used in some ancient titles.

CORN LAWS   Laws regulating the English corn trade, particularly restricting the import of wheat, thus ensuring the producer always got a good price; but in times of shortage it caused high bread prices and suffering among the poor. Repealed 1846.

COTTAR   Peasant working on the land.

CURIA REGIS   The King's Council.

DEBUTANTE   Girl "coming out," or being presented in society.

DEMESNE   That part of an estate occupied and worked by the owner and not rented out to tenants.

DEVICE   Heraldic design or emblem.

DIGGERS   An extreme seventeenth-century sect who called for the redistribution of land in a fairer way.

DIVINE RIGHT   Belief that a monarch ruled by the wish of God.

DOMESDAY BOOK   The great survey of English landowning and holding made on the orders of William I, 1086–87.

DUKE   The highest of the hereditary titles of the peerage, outside the royal family.

EARL   One of the ranks of the English peerage.

EARL MARSHALL   Officer who is head of the College of Arms.

ENCLOSURES   The fencing in of common agricultural or heath land to make it private property. In England there were marked enclosure movements in the thirteenth and eighteenth centuries.

ENFEOFFMENT   Giving a fief or landholding to someone subordinate in rank.

ESTATE DUTY   Tax payable on a landlord's estate or possessions when he dies.

FIEF   Feudal land holding.

FLANDERS   A distinct territory in medieval times in the area of present-day north Belgium and southern Holland.

GOTHIC REVIVAL   Architectural style popular in the eighteenth and nineteenth centuries. It imitated medieval Gothic styles.

GRAND TOUR   The extensive tour of Europe regarded as an important part of the education of young English aristocrats.

HANOVERIANS   Members of the German house of Hanover, which became the British ruling house with the accession of George I to the British throne in 1714.

HERALDRY   The recording of genealogies and the devising of ceremonial bearings for a member of the nobility.

HIDE   A medieval measurement of land, varying between 60 and 120 acres.

HUNDRED   Subdivision of a county, particularly common in medieval times.

IMPEACH   Charge with a crime, usually when an official of the government has committed treason or is corrupt.

INDENTURE   Contract or agreement between two people, usually binding one to work for the other for a certain length of time.

JESUIT   Member of the Society of Jesus, a powerful Roman Catholic religious order founded in 1540 by Ignatius Loyola.

KNIGHT   Title usually bestowed by the monarch in recognition of service to the crown. Today it is more likely to be for service to the government or the community.

LANCASTRIAN   Member or follower of the House of Lancaster during the Wars of the Roses.

LEVELLER   Member of an extreme republican faction (1647–9) advocating complete social and religious equality.

LIFE PEER   Person granted a title which cannot be passed onto his heir.

LIVERY AND MAINTENANCE   The practice whereby great noblemen provided the clothing, food and lodging for their retainers.

LORD LIEUTENANT   The Crown's appointed representative in English counties.

MAGNATE   Someone of great wealth and influence.

MANOR   Medieval feudal estate.

MARCHER LORDS   The noblemen who controlled the border lands between England and Wales.

MARQUESS   Rank of the British peerage second only in importance to dukes.

MASQUE An entertainment popular in 16th and 17th century England, it combined verse, music, mime and tableaux.
MERCENARIES Hired soldiers serving a country or lord not his own in return for payment.
MERCIA Anglo-Saxon kingdom in central England from the 6th to the 9th centuries.
MONOPOLY Exclusive possession of trade in a particular commodity or business.
"NOBLESSE OBLIGE" Privileged position that entails responsibility.
NORMANS Inhabitants of Normandy, France; people who came to England from there after the Conquest of England by William of Normandy in 1066.
PATENT Official document granting a right, privilege or title.
PATRONAGE Help, encouragement and/or protection given to someone less influential or rich than the giver.
PLANTAGENET Member of the English royal dynasty founded by Geoffrey, count of Anjou and father of Henry II (1154–89). They ruled England and much of western France.
PRIMOGENITURE The custom by which estates were handed down intact to the eldest son.
PRIVY COUNCIL Council or committee which advises the Crown on affairs of state. It has little power now, but from the 13th to 18th centuries exercised much influence in the running of the country.
ROTTEN BOROUGH A parliamentary constituency which had the right to elect Members of Parliament even though its population was too small to meet the legal requirements. The elected members were usually nominees of the landowners. These boroughs were abolished in 1832.
SCUTAGE Tax paid by feudal landowner instead of personal military service.
SEASON, the, The time of greatest social activity among the aristocracy.
SERVITIA DEBITA Obligatory number of knights owed by feudal lord to king in Norman times.
SHIRE Anglo-Saxon administrative district, similar to counties.
STATELY HOME Ancestral home, usually large, of a member of the aristocracy.
STEWARD Official who ran his lord's estate, often in the absence of the lord.
STUARTS Member of the Scottish dynasty which ruled Scotland from 1371–1714 and England from 1603–49 and 1660–1714.
SUB-INFEUDATION The practice of tenants-in-chief to give part of the lands they had received from the Crown to lesser noblemen in return for feudal services.
SUMPTUARY LAWS Laws regulating the clothes and food that each class of society could wear or eat.
TENANT-IN-CHIEF The great lords and nobles who received their

lands from the king.

THEGN   In Anglo-Saxon times a soldier owed by a lord to the King in return for every five hides held.

TORIES   The fore-runners of today's Conservative party. They opposed attempts in 1679 to exclude James II from the succession and became the party to support the Anglican church, the hereditary monarchy and the rights of the landed nobility.

TOURNAMENT   A mock battle between armed and mounted knights popular in the Middle Ages.

TUDORS   Members of the dynasty ruling England 1485–1603.

VILLEIN   Feudal workman bound to work for his lord in return for his own small piece of land.

VIRGATE   A land measurement used in medieval times.

VISCOUNT   The fourth of the five orders of British peerage.

WARDSHIP   Guardianship of people or lands, often exercised by medieval lords over their dependents.

WHIGS   In 1679 opposed succession of James II, developed into the radical, reforming party in 18th and 19th century British politics.

WITAN   Members of the Anglo-Saxon council or Witenagemot.

WRIT   Command or summons usually issued by the sovereign.

YOUNG ENGLAND MOVEMENT   Radical Tory movement in 1830s, advocating government based on monarchy, aristocracy and church, but protecting the working class.

YORKISTS   Members or supporters of the house of York in the Wars of the Roses.

Table of Dates

1066	Battle of Hastings, victory of William of Normandy who becomes William I of England. Norman knights who came with William granted fiefs of land by the king. The English aristocracy gradually becomes Anglo-Norman.
1086	Domesday Book – the survey of landholding and land ownership in England carried out on the orders of William I.
1087	Accession of William II, second son of William I.
1100	Accession of Henry I, third son of William I.
1135	Stephen comes to the throne. Strife breaks out between Stephen and his cousin Matilda. Nobility build castles for self-protection. Power of the barons increases due to civil strife.
1154	Henry II ascends throne. Enforces payment of scutage by his knights. This pays for his mercenary armies in his wars with France.
1189	Richard I becomes king. Is absent from England crusading in the Holy Land for much of his reign.
1199	John succeeds his brother, Richard I. John has little control over the nobility.
1215	John forced by his barons to sign Magna Carta, confirming their feudal rights.
1216	Henry III succeeds his father John on the English throne.
1258	Provisions of Oxford. Rebel barons try to force the king to rule through a council of the most powerful magnates.
1264	Barons' revolt lead by Simon de Montfort. Defeat king at the Battle of Lewes.
1272	Accession of Edward I.
1307	Edward II comes to the throne. The barons resented the power of his favourites, to whom Edward left the running of the country.
1326	Roger Mortimer, allied with Isabella, Edward's wife, invades, deposes Edward who is murdered.
1327	Edward III comes to the throne, is at first dominated by his mother and the Mortimer faction.
1348–9	The Black Death.
1377	Richard II comes to the throne. Until he came of age in

	1383 the country ruled by John of Gaunt.
1381	Peasants' Revolt.
1399	Richard deposed by Henry IV, Henry puts down baronial revolts in 1403 and 1405.
1413	Henry V succeeds his father, Henry IV.
1422	Accession of Henry VI. The dukes of Gloucester and Lancaster acted as Regents during his minority.
1454	Duke of York appointed Protector of the realm due to Henry's increasing attacks of insanity.
1455	Outbreak of the civil wars of the Roses, between the rival ducal houses of York and Lancaster.
1461	Edward IV comes to the throne on the deposition of Henry VI.
1470	Henry briefly restored to power through help of the Earl of Warwick, the "Kingmaker." Henry murdered the following year.
1483	Edward V succeeds to throne.
1483	Richard III, uncle of Edward V and popularly regarded as ordering his murder, becomes king. He never had full support from the nobles and was defeated by Henry Tudor at the Battle of Bosworth in 1485.
1485	Henry Tudor becomes Henry VII of England after defeating Richard III. Nobility reduced by the Wars of the Roses and attainders. Henry does much to end livery and maintenance, the basis of aristocratic power.
1501	For the first time the King's council contained more commoners than noblemen.
1509	Henry VIII comes to the throne. His Dissolution of the Monasteries increased the land and wealth at the disposal of the Crown, which now became a greater landowner than any of the noble families.
1547	Edward VI came to the throne at the age of 10. His reign dominated by power struggle between the Dukes of Somerset and Northumberland.
1553	Mary, daughter of Henry VIII and Catherine of Aragon, becomes Queen.
1558	Elizabeth I, Mary's half-sister, succeeds to the throne. By a firm policy of creating few new titles and keeping governmental power away from the old aristocracy she made sure the nobility could no longer rival the Crown.
1603	Accession of James I of England and VI of Scotland. He created and sold many new titles as a means of raising money.
1625	Charles I succeeds his father, and continues his policy of creating titles for sale.
1642–49	Civil War shows nobility no longer has military superiority.
1649–59	The period of the Commonwealth and Protectorate under Cromwell.

1660	The Restoration – Charles II restored to the English throne.
1685	James II, second son of Charles I, succeeds his brother Charles. Sympathetic to the Roman Catholics, he was disliked by many of the newer nobility who had gained their lands after the Reformation and Dissolution of the monasteries.
1689	William and Mary, James II's daughter and son-in-law, come to the throne at the invitation of the dissatisfied upper classes. James flees to France.
1702	Anne becomes Queen.
1714	On death of Anne without heirs, throne passes to George, elector of Hanover.
1727	George II succeeds his father.
1760	George III becomes king. Insane from 1811, the country was ruled by his son, the Prince of Wales. Throughout the Hanoverian period, the nobility were gradually extending their interests, and their fortunes, in trade and industry. Pitt makes many new peers.
1820	George IV becomes king in name as well as fact, having ruled England since 1811, due to his father's insanity.
1830	William IV, brother of George IV, becomes King.
1832	Reform Act. It slightly extended the franchise and abolished the rotten boroughs through which the nobles had been able to control Parliament.
1837	Victoria becomes Queen of England.
1846	Repeal of the Corn Laws. End of protection for home grown wheat. Effect on great landowners felt twenty years later.
1867	The Second Reform Act.
1872	The Second Domesday Survey. A survey carried out by Lord Derby to show that the land was now owned by the common people. In fact it showed that they only held about one-fifth of the country. The aristocrats still owned England.
1880	County Councils set up, finally ending the local governmental influence of the great landowners.
1901	Edward VII.
1910	George V becomes king.
1911	Parliament Act, limiting the power of the House of Lords, and thus the hereditary peers.
1914–18	The First World War greatly contributed to the break up of many of the old estates. Death duties, deaths of heirs in the war and high taxation made it more profitable to sell.
1936	Edward VIII, abdicated.
1936	George VI, second son of George V, succeeds his brother.
1939–45	Second World War.
1952	Elizabeth II come to the throne.
1958	Elizabeth II announces abolition of presentation of debutantes at court.
1958	Introduction of life peerages.

1963	Peerage Act, allowing peers to renounce their titles, and so, if they are Members of Parliament, to remain in the House of Commons. Previously, on succession to a title the M.P. had to resign and take his seat in the House of Lords. This was final acknowledgment of the supremacy of the House of Commons.

Further Reading

Chapter 1
Baker, Timothy, *The Normans*, Cassell 1966
Douglas, David, *William the Conqueror*, Eyre & Spottiswoode 1966
Labarge, Margaret, *A Baronial Household in the Thirteenth Century*, Eyre & Spottiswoode 1965
Matthew, D. J. A., *The Norman Conquest*, Batsford 1966
Painter, Sydney, *Studies in the History of the English Feudal Barony*, Johns Hopkins Press 1944
Round, J. H., *Geoffrey de Mandeville*, Longmans 1892
Stenton, F. M., *The First Century of English Feudalism*, O.U.P. 1932

Chapter 2
Bagley, J. J., *Life in Medieval England*, Batsford 1960
Du Boulay, F. R. H., *An Age of Ambition*, Nelson 1970
Kendall, P. M., *The Yorkist Age*, George Allen & Unwin 1962
Kendall, P. M., *Warwick the Kingmaker*, George Allen & Unwin 1957
McFarlane, K. B., *The Nobility of Later Medieval England*, O.U.P. 1973
Rickert, Edith, *Chaucer's World*, Columbia University Press 1948
Storey, R. L., *The End of the House of Lancaster*, Barrie & Rockliff 1966

Chapter 3
Bindoff, S. T., *Tudor England*, Penguin 1950
Handover, P. M., *The Second Cecil*, Eyre & Spottiswoode 1959
Harrison, G. B. (Ed.), *Advice to his Son by Henry Percy*, Ernest Benn 1930
Lander, J. R., "Attainder and Forfeiture," *Historical Journal* IV, 1961
Rowse, A. L., *The England of Elizabeth*, Macmillan 1950
Scott Thomson, G., *Two Centuries of Family History*, Longmans 1930
Williams, Penry, *Life in Tudor England*, Batsford 1964

Chapter 4
Ashley, Maurice, *Life in Stuart England*, Batsford, 1964
Firth, C. H., *The House of Lords During the Civil War*, Longmans 1910
Scott Thomson, G., *Life in a Noble Household*, Cape 1937
Stone, Lawrence, *The Crisis of the Aristocracy*, O.U.P. 1965
Tawney, R. H., "The Rise of the Gentry," *Economic History Review*, 1941

Chapter 5
Carswell, John, *The South Sea Bubble*, Cresset Press 1960

Cecil, Lord David, *The Young Melbourne*, Constable 1939
Hobhouse, Christopher, *Fox*, Constable 1934
Mingay, G. E., *English Landed Society in the Eighteenth Century*, Routledge 1963
Plumb, J. H., *England in the Eighteenth Century*, Penguin 1950
Plumb, J. H., *Sir Robert Walpole*, Cresset Press 1956
Turberville, A. S., *English Men and Manners in the Eighteenth Century*, Oxford 1926
White, R. J., *Life in Regency England*, Batsford 1963

Chapter 6

Blake, Robert, *Disraeli*, Eyre & Spottiswoode 1966
Cecil, Robert, *Life in Edwardian England*, Batsford 1969
Emerson, R. W., *English Traits*, Harvard University Press 1966
Guttsman, W. L., *The English Ruling Class*, Weidenfeld & Nicolson 1969
Longford, Elizabeth, *Wellington*, Weidenfeld & Nicolson 1970
Reader, W. J., *Life in Victorian England*, Batsford 1964
Rhodes James, Robert, *Lord Randolph Churchill*, Weidenfeld & Nicolson 1959
Thompson, F. M. L., *English Landed Society in the Nineteenth Century*, Routledge 1963

Chapter 7

Bedford, John, Duke of, *Silver Plated Spoon*, Cassell 1959
Egremont, John, *Wyndham and Children First*, Macmillan 1968
Macmillan, Gerald, *Honours for Sale*, Richards Press 1954
Mitford, Nancy, *Noblesse Oblige*, Hamish Hamilton 1956
Percy, Eustace, *Some Memories*, Eyre & Spottiswoode 1958
Perrott, Roy, *The Aristocrats*, Weidenfeld & Nicolson 1968
Pine, L. G., *Ramshackledom*, Secker & Warburg 1962
Sinclair, Andrew, *The Last of the Best*, Weidenfeld & Nicolson 1969

For a comprehensive guide to the homes of the aristocracy in England the reader is referred to *Historic Houses, Castles and Gardens in Great Britain and Ireland* published annually by A.B.C. Travel Guides Ltd.

Index

Anne, Queen, 73
Army reforms, 102
Arts, patronage of, 32, 33, 53, 70, 87, 96, 111
Attainders, 35

Baring, Alexander, Lord Ashburton, 96, 103
"Bastard Feudalism", 24
Bath, Marquesses of, 93, 95, 96, 110, 112, 113, 114, 115
Black Death, 22, 25
Bridgwater, Earls and Dukes of, 67, 76, 88, 94
Brydges, James, Duke of Chandos, 74, 76, 82, 84, 86, 87

Cambridge, University of, 30, 33, 45, 70, 103
Canals, 76
Castles, 9–10, 14, 17, 18, 19, 27, 28, 65
Cavendish family, Earls and Dukes of Devonshire, 69, 84, 85, 88, 91, 95, 97, 98, 109, 110, 111, 112, 114, 115
Cecil family, Earls and Marquesses of Salisbury, 37, 38, 41, 43, 45, 47, 51, 55, 65, 67, 69, 98, 104, 106, 109
Charles I, 55, 56, 70, 72
Charles II, 55, 58, 63, 70, 76
Chartism, 94
Chivalry, 16, 19, 22, 27, 30
Churchill family, Dukes of Marlborough, 73, 74, 86, 96, 97, 102, 106, 108
Civil Service, 101, 102
Coke family, Earls of Leicester of Holkham, 76, 77, 88, 103, 113
Corn Laws, repeal of, 91, 92, 97, 106
Council of the North, 29, 36

Country houses: Alnwick, 17, 92, 94, 95, 113; Ashridge, 94; Battle Abbey, 95; Beaulieu, 113; Belvoir Castle, 87, 94, 110, 113; Blenheim, 74, 86, 113; Cannons, 74, 86; Castle Howard, 86; Chatsworth, 69, 95, 111, 113; Chenies, 43; Cheshunt, 43; Chiswick House, 86, 87; Cliveden, 111; Cobham Hall, 87; Cowdray, 43; Eaton Hall, 94, 95, 113; Frogmore, 95; Hardwicke Hall, 41; Hatfield House, 69, 111; Holdenby, 41, 42, 43, 47; Holkham Hall, 113; Houghton, 86; Hughenden, 103; Kenilworth, 47; Knole, 95; Longleat, 95, 110, 113, 116; Petworth, 76, 87, 94, 99; Raby, 95, 113; Syon House, 74; Theobalds, 41, 43, 69; Waddesdon, 103; Waltham, 43; Wentworth, 76, 86; Wilton House, 93, 113, 114; Woburn, 37, 66, 69, 70, 113; Wollaton, 41
Cromwell, 65, 72
Crusades, 15
Curia Regis, 9, 13, 15, 17, 25, 27, 36

Death Duties, 99, 110, 114
De Donis, Statute, 19
Disraeli, Benjamin, Lord Beaconsfield, 88, 92, 93, 99, 100, 103
Divine Right, 38
Domesday Book, 10
Douglas-Home, Sir Alec, 109, 110, 115
Dudley, Robert, Earl of Leicester, 37, 38, 44, 47, 52

Education, 29–30, 45, 70, 84, 99, 103, 110, 115
Edward I, 9, 19, 21, 22, 25
Edward II, 21
Edward III, 20, 21, 22, 23, 25, 27
Edward IV, 26, 36
Edward VI, 39
Edward VII, 101
Elizabeth I, 37, 38, 39, 40, 43, 47, 51, 53, 56
Elizabeth II, 107, 112, 116
Enclosures, 76, 78

Eton College, 30, 70, 71, 84, 103, 114, 115, 116
Fashions, 19, 27, 44, 45, 48, 49, 50, 64, 67–8, 86
First World War, 99, 110, 112
Food, 19, 28, 68–9, 87
Furniture, 27, 44, 45, 46, 86

Gardens, 86
Gambling clubs, 85, 86, 114
Gaunt, John of, 22, 23, 25, 32
George I, 73, 75, 79
George II, 73
George III, 85
George V, 107
Gladstone, W. E., 102, 106
Grand Tour, 45, 70, 82, 84
Grosvenor family, Dukes and Earls of Westminster, 74–5, 77, 94, 108, 110, 112
Gwyn, Nell, 55, 58, 63

Harold, King, 9, 11
Hastings, Battle of, 10
Hatton, Sir Christopher, 37, 41, 43, 44, 47, 53
Hawking, 17
Henry I, 11, 13, 14
Henry II, 13, 14, 15, 16, 22
Henry III, 16, 17, 21
Henry V, 27, 28, 31
Henry VI, 23, 26
Henry VII, 34, 35, 36
Henry VIII, 36, 39
Heraldry, 16, 41, 111
Horse racing, 87–88, 95
Howard family, Dukes of Norfolk, 39, 47, 55, 91, 111
Hunting, 17, 19, 33, 95, 96, 106, 114
Hyde, Edward, Earl of Clarendon, 55, 56

Indenture System, 22, 23, 36
Inns of Court, 31, 37, 45

James I, 8, 37, 54, 55, 67
James II, 65, 72, 73
Jews, 22, 106
John, King, 13, 15
Jones, Inigo, 66, 69
Jousts, 21
Justice, 15, 24, 29, 32, 36

Labour Party, 107, 108, 112, 113
Lambton family, Earls of Durham, 82, 98, 103, 116
Livery and Maintenance, 23, 24, 35, 39

127

Lloyd George, David, 98, 106, 107, 112

Macmillan, Harold, 108, 109, 111
Magna Carta, 15
Mary, Queen, 39
Mary, Queen of Scots, 55, 106
Matilda, Empress, 14
Melbourne, Lord, 84
Monopolies, 22, 51, 67
Montagu family, 66, 67, 68, 113
Montfort, Simon de, 16, 17, 18, 19, 21

Neville family, Earls of Warwick, 21, 23, 24, 26, 31, 39, 51
Newcastle, Dukes of, 73, 75, 82, 110
New Domesday Survey, 91
New Model Army, 65
Noblesse Oblige, 99, 115, 116
Northcliffe, Lord, 106

Order of the Garter, 21
Ordericus Vitalis, 11, 13
Oxford, University of, 30, 31, 33, 45, 70, 84, 102, 103, 110, 115, 116

Parliament, 25, 32, 33, 35, 36, 39, 55, 56, 65, 77, 80, 81, 82, 84, 86, 91, 96, 107, 108, 116
Parliament Act, 106, 108
Paston family, 24
Peasants' Revolt, 21, 22, 33
Peerage Act, 109
Pembroke, Earls of, 92, 93, 113, 114, 115
Percy family, Earls of Northumberland, 17, 22, 23, 24, 27, 30, 35, 39, 45, 47, 53, 70, 74, 88, 92, 93, 110, 115
Peterloo Massacre, 88, 90
Pitt, William the elder, Earl of Chatham, 74, 75, 82, 84
Pole, de la, family, Earls and Dukes of Suffolk, 22, 23, 24, 28, 35, 40, 108
Portland, Earls and Dukes of, 22, 94, 98, 103, 112
Primogeniture, 7, 8, 26, 73, 75, 116
Prodigy houses, 41, 43, 44
Provisions of Oxford, 17
"Progresses," 47

Quia Emptores, statute, 23

Railways, 92, 93, 94, 97, 98, 110
Reform Acts, 91, 92, 106, 116
Reformation, 36, 72
Richard I, 15, 17
Richard II, 13, 21
Richmond, Duke of, 73, 89, 91
Rothschild family, 96, 98, 99, 103
Round Table, 16, 21
Russell family, Earls and Dukes of Bedford, 23, 37, 43, 44, 47, 51, 65, 66, 67, 69, 70, 72, 73, 75, 77, 79, 81, 87, 94, 111, 113
Rutland, Dukes and Earls of, 66, 70, 87, 94, 95, 99, 110

Saxon risings, 10, 14
Scutage, 14, 15, 22
Second World War, 111, 112

Servitia debita, 12
Shaftesbury, Earls of, 65, 99
Six Acts, 88
South Sea Bubble, 75, 76, 77
Spas, 70, 71, 87
Stanley family, Earls and Dukes of Derby, 45, 56, 91, 92, 106, 112
Star Chamber, 35
Stephen, King, 13, 14, 15
Sumptuary Laws, 35–6, 40

Theatre, 58, 63, 65, 67, 75
Tilting, 47, 53
Tories, 67, 88
Tournaments, 16, 17, 21, 27, 47
Town houses, 23, 47, 51, 66, 69–70, 77, 78, 83, 84, 94, 95, 112
Trade and industry, 66, 67, 75, 76, 92, 98, 106

Victoria, Queen, 101
Villiers, George, Duke of Buckingham, 55, 56, 57, 67

Walpole, Sir Robert, 76, 81, 82, 86
Wars of the Roses, 8, 26, 35, 65, 106
Wedgwood Benn, Anthony, 109
Wellington, Duke of, 88, 91, 92, 103, 112, 116
Whigs, 67, 88
William I, 8, 9, 10, 11, 12, 14, 22
William II, 13
William III, 72, 73, 79

Young England Movement, 99

ACKNOWLEDGEMENTS

The author and publishers would like to thank the following for loaning pictures used in this book: *Black and white,* Giraudon, p. 9 (top); Mansell Collection, frontispiece, pp. 15 (top), 16 (middle left), 17, 20, 25, 38 (left), 39 (top right), 42, 49, 50, 52 (right), 64, 68 (top right), 71 (top), 76 (bottom), 79, 80, 83, 86 (bottom), 88, 89 (top), 90–91, 92 (top left, top right), 96 (middle), 97 (left), 99, 101, 102, 104–5, 108; Radio Times Hulton Picture Library, pp. 10, 19 (bottom), 24 (top), 28, 31, 37 (bottom), 46 (top), 51 (top), 52 (left), 74 (right), 78 (top), 82 (top), 84, 94 (middle), 92 (bottom), 93 (top), 100, 111 (bottom); British Museum, pp. 11–13, 15 (bottom), 16 (top left and right), 19 (top and middle), 21, 27 (bottom), 29, 32, 33, 57 (bottom); Department of the Environment, pp. 18, 69 (bottom), 82 (bottom), 95 (top); Mary Evans Picture Library, pp. 27 (top), 86 (top), 95 (bottom); National Portrait Gallery, pp. 34, 38 (right), 39 (left), 48 (right), 54, 56, 57 (top), 58, 59, 74 (left), 75 (top), 77 (top right), 81, 93 (bottom), 94 (bottom), 97 (right), 106, 107; British Tourist Authority, pp. 37 (top), 112; Bodleian Library, Oxford, p. 39 (bottom); National Monuments Record, pp. 41, 71 (bottom), 87 (bottom); John Freeman, pp. 43, 75 (bottom), 89 (bottom), 96 (bottom), 97 (top); The London Museum, pp. 44, 51 (bottom), 78 (bottom), 87 (top); Victoria and Albert Museum, p. 46 (bottom); Keystone Press Agency, pp. 109, 110, 111 (top), 112, 115. *Colour,* Tate Gallery, jacket; John Freeman, pp. 60, 61 (bottom), 62.